Dearest
Dena,

Love & Blessing

Calli

Keep Shining

Also By Christine Kloser

A DAILY DOSE OF LOVE
Everyday Inspiration to Help You Remember
What Your Heart Already Knows

PEBBLES IN THE POND
Transforming the World One Person at a Time
(Wave One)

CONSCIOUS ENTREPRENEURS
A Radical New Approach to Purpose, Passion and Profit

THE FREEDOM FORMULA
How to Put Soul in Your Business
and Money in Your Bank

INSPIRATION TO REALIZATION
Real Women Reveal Proven Strategies for Personal,
Business, Financial and Spiritual Fulfillment

PEBBLES

in the

POND

Transforming the World
One Person at a Time

~Wave Two~

TRANSFORMATION BOOKS
York, PA

Pebbles in the Pond: Transforming the World One Person at a Time (Wave Two)

Published by:
Transformation Books
211 Pauline Drive #513
York, PA 17402
www.TransformationBooks.com

ISBN: 978-0-9851407-5-5
Library of Congress Control No: 2013935686

Cover design by Sarah Barrie
Layout and typesetting by Ranilo Cabo
Editor: Marlene Oulton, www.MarleneOulton.com
Proofreader: Gwen Hoffnagle

Printed in the United States of America

A portion of the proceeds from the sale of this book will be donated to the causes the publisher supports.

Help Me Be...

Strong enough to be vulnerable.

Wise enough to realize how little I know.

Loving enough to embrace my "enemy."

Tender enough to be powerful.

Smart enough to realize I can't do it alone.

Brilliant enough to shine the light of others.

Doubtful enough to know the power of faith.

Courageous enough to share my truth.

~Christine Kloser

Table of Contents

Introduction   1

"Everything's Fine"… and Other Lies
I've Told Myself   5
     Christine Kloser

It All Starts with Me   11
     Noni Boon

Intentional Transformation and Your   19
Power to Be Free
     MaryJo Briggs, MScEd

The Two Yous: How and Why to Awaken to
Your Soul   29
     Janis Fossette Butler, BA

Journey of Self to Soul   39
     Tara Chatterton

**The Art of Becoming a Magnet
for Transformation**   45
Bo Eason

ChristIAm, Who We Are in Truth   51
Marilyn Garrett

**From Victim to Empowered Agent for
Transformation and Love**   59
Bridgit Charandura Gooden

All Is Well with My Soul   69
Christina Haas

**Triumph Alchemy – Transforming Life's
Challenges into Golden Accomplishments**   77
Vivian Hanai

**The Alchemy of Connection – Through Life,
Death, and Rebirth**   85
Katrine Legg Hauger
Certified Constellator, Lawyer

The Secrets and Shadows of Lost Understanding   95
Angela Hiroshima, CECF

The Making of a Transformational Soul   105
Barbara Marx Hubbard

Transform Your Trauma into Your Triumph   111
Calli D. Meister

From Devastation to Celebration!   119
Fiona Miller, BSc

Paving the Path to Transformation   127
Lisa Nichols

Wake Up, Sleeping Beauty   135
Rosie Quigley

Safari into the Soul   145
Mia Rose

The Vision of Transformation   153
Jeff Saxton

Out of the Darkness and Then Some   161
Marcia Ullett, MA, LMFT, CPC

It's Not About You   169
Neale Donald Walsch

Becoming a Contributing Author   179

Connect With Christine Kloser   181

About Christine Kloser   183

Introduction

"A small body of determined spirits fired by an unquenchable faith in their mission can alter the course of history."

~ Gandhi

THANK YOU FOR FOLLOWING THE WHISPER in your heart to pick up this book and crack open the cover. My guess is – like the contributors to this book – you've been on a powerful, transformational journey that sometimes joyously surprises you and other times throws you an unexpected curve ball that knocks you to your knees.

Perhaps as you read this you're in the middle of the most challenging time of your life. Or maybe you've just come through a difficult situation with a renewed sense of faith and hope. Perhaps you have a niggling sense that a growth opportunity is lurking around the corner waiting for you, but you just don't know what it is… yet.

No matter where you stand right now on your path, I trust that since you're here – taking time to read this book – you believe in the concept of a "pebble in the pond" and share in the vision of a world that is transformed one person at a time.

While world transformation may seem like a far-fetched dream, the truth I've come to know is that as we transform as individuals, we *do* make a difference in the lives of those around us. And if you've ever thrown a stone in a still pond, you know that one single splash sends ripples outward in every direction, creating more and more ripples. It's the same thing when that "splash" is the impact of your life and how you live it each and every day – the impact expands.

It doesn't matter if you're a leading-edge entrepreneur, schoolteacher, mom, rocket scientist, doctor, writer, healer, manager, salesperson, nurse, volunteer, retiree, or anything else; your life – and how you live it – can be a force for good in our world. Every person has the power to make a difference, including you, and that's exactly what this book is about.

At this time in history we are on the precipice of experiencing the new world many people have been dreaming about – a world filled with love, cooperation, contribution, service, community, and abundance for all. And there are a growing number of people who are doing all they can to heal themselves, become a part of the solution (simply by being who they truly and authentically are), and bring more light and love into the world.

In the pages of this book you'll meet such visionary leaders and world-changers. You may recognize some of the contributors as bestselling authors and leading entrepreneurs. Others aren't as well known, yet their stories are testaments to the power of one person's transformational journey to send ripples of good into the world.

I personally feel so blessed to receive the gift of working closely with most of the contributors to this book. We've gathered together over the course of eight months to birth this book in service to you. As you discover each contributor's story, you'll see why I consider it a blessing to call them my clients, soul travelers, and friends. *Pebbles in the Pond* is only possible because of the love and light they bring to the world.

Some chapters will make you cry, while others will make you laugh. Some will touch your heart deeply, while others will inspire you to think differently. Some chapters will be difficult to read as you hear of the challenges a few of the authors have faced that nobody should ever have to live through. And others will offer you a heartfelt reassurance that if they can do it (whatever the "it" is), you can, too.

So as you proceed through this book, don't feel the need to read the chapters in order. Chances are as you peruse the table of contents or randomly flip open the pages, you will receive exactly the message that is meant for you in that moment. Let your experience reading *Pebbles in the Pond* be exactly right for you.

Above all else, let the stories in this book bathe you in love, compassion, understanding, and inspiration to transform your challenges and struggles (large or small) into beautiful blessings for yourself and others.

You never know what miracle may happen as a result of reading one of these stories. In fact, this book series in and of itself is evidence of the miraculous grace that appeared during the most challenging time of my life. In Wave One of *Pebbles in the Pond,* the title of my chapter is "The Best 'Worst' Time of My Life."

It was the worst time because I was going through personal bankruptcy and a very challenging dissolution of a business partnership, unsure about how I was going to support my family and questioning everything about who I knew myself to be. Saying I felt like a failure puts it mildly. Yet that challenging time opened my heart in ways I never knew possible – and one of the many "gifts in the challenge" was the concept for this book series.

With this — Wave Two of *Pebbles in the Pond* — the ripples continue to encompass and empower you to be who you are here to be... and to let your light shine!

On behalf of myself and all of the contributing authors to both "Waves" in this series, we send you our deepest blessings that this book delivers the inspiration and transformation your soul is seeking. May you be guided by grace.

Love and blessings,

Christine Kloser,
Spiritual Guide ~ Award Winning Author
Transformational Book Coach ~ Publisher

"Everything's Fine"… and Other Lies I've Told Myself

Christine Kloser

HOW MANY TIMES HAVE YOU SAID "everything's fine" when it wasn't really true? If you're anything like me you've said it too many times to count, and you've felt the negative repercussions of this small but powerful statement in your life.

Ever since I can remember, I've had the disposition of "everything's fine." If someone in my life, especially when I was a child, was struggling with a major difficulty or facing a challenge, my family seemed to disapprove of the person rather than being empathetic about the situation they were in. It was taboo if someone we knew was seeing a "shrink." (That was what my family called a psychotherapist back then.) Nobody really talked about cancer (which three of my five immediate family members have survived) or any other life-changing illnesses or problems. Everything was always "fine" in our world. Except it wasn't — at least not with me.

Of course I can see this behavior clearly now as an adult woman who is on a spiritual and healing path, committed to shifting my own consciousness. But as a child I didn't know a different way of being.

I believe that my parents, given the circumstances of their youth, loved me and my sisters dearly, and truly did an amazing job raising us. There was never abuse, addiction, or any type of destructive behavior in our home. We always had a warm home-cooked meal on the table every night. I never heard complaints about "Mom's taxi" driving to and from the ice skating rink where I trained, nor did I ever perform or compete without my parents cheering from the audience. They paid for my private college education, planned family vacations every summer to Cape Cod or Florida, and made sure my physical needs were always met. Sure, I was grounded when I misbehaved, and we had our fair share of arguments, but overall I believed everything was fine. So as I began my journey into adulthood, I proceeded in my life as though the "everything's fine" philosophy was the truth.

Nothing was a big deal.

Doing terrible in college and trying to fit in by drinking way too much and way too often... no big deal. Moving 3,000 miles across the country after graduating from college to escape post-college reality... no big deal. Leaving behind the boyfriend I had for two years to make that move... no big deal. Having my fair share of bad romantic relationships... no big deal. Facing the aftermath of a breakup... no big deal. Taking on a new business that was far beyond my financial capacity... no big deal. Building another business despite an inner niggling that it wasn't right for me... no big deal. Trying to do everything on my own without asking for help when I needed it... no big deal. Acting as if everything was fine when it wasn't... no big deal. I'm sure by now you get the picture.

I was so emotionally shut down that I can recall a moment in 2003 when I began to see just how out of touch I was with my own heart. A dear friend of mine was going through a big transformation in her life that was the most difficult thing she'd ever experienced. We were supposed to get together to take a walk on the beach, but she called to tell me she wasn't up to it because she was having a very difficult time emotionally.

I loved this friend and cared very much for her well-being. Yet I remember when she made the statement about her feelings, I felt in my being that I had no understanding of what it meant to have a difficult day on an emotional level. I honestly didn't comprehend why she couldn't just get herself together and join me on the beach. How could her emotions keep her from doing something as simple as taking a walk with a friend?

When I think back to that moment now, it breaks my heart. It was then that I began to realize that everything really wasn't fine – and that it wasn't okay for me to continue to deny my own emotional well-being and just keep going, and going, and going. Going where? I didn't even know where "there" was most of the time. But as long as I was in motion, always busy, with a to-do list longer than Super Woman could conquer, I was "fine."

Constant activity and busyness kept me on emotional autopilot… or shall I say "emotionally shut-down" autopilot.

I had friends and a wonderful husband… yet no emotional intimacy. I was missing out on the gift of fully experiencing all of life's ups (and downs) by not even being aware of the world of emotions that would help me feel more alive and connected than I ever dreamed possible. Life can feel really "flat" when the only thing you know how to feel is fine.

So that day when my friend cancelled our walk was when I unconsciously set my foot on a different path. I say unconsciously because ten years later I can see it clearly, but at the time I wasn't aware enough to make the conscious choice to live my life differently and explore my own emotional landscape. You may be asking how I know that my foot got set on a different path that day. I can say this for two different reasons. One is because that memory is so vivid to me. It was the first time I saw my inability to comprehend someone having an emotional life. Two, looking back from where I stand today, it's almost impossible to recognize who I was then. I've grown, evolved, and opened my heart in so many ways over the years, especially the past two.

So how did I – and how can you – break the cycle of "everything's fine"? Let me share a little of my own journey to breaking free of the "fine syndrome" in the hopes of helping you with yours.

First I want to say that I wouldn't wish my journey on anyone. It was gut-wrenchingly difficult. Granted it was worth every moment of the pain and suffering because I love who I am and where I am in my life today… but wow, it was tough!

I finally began to consciously "wake up" as my life and business came crumbling down around me. Remember I said I'd built a business that didn't feel quite right? Well, that business slowly crumbled for a few years. It really is impossible to sustain a business (at least a fulfilling and successful one) if, in your heart, you know it's not totally right and not fully aligned with who you are. The slow crumble came to a crash in June of 2010 when, after years of struggle, my husband and I made the decision to file for bankruptcy. Talk about everything *not* being fine.

My biggest fear in making this heartbreaking decision was what people would think of me. They would now *know* (beyond any shadow of a doubt) that things were anything but fine! Of course, I was terrified of not knowing how I'd support my family, but the fear of this failure filled my heart and mind. Who was I if I wasn't fine?

Ahh… that question, and the figurative two-by-four to the head realization that everything *wasn't* fine, shocked me out of my emotional haze. For months I worked on sharing more of my journey, talking with people I trusted about what was going on, and healing myself through this time. Then, just as the bankruptcy proceedings were about to be finalized, I received another blow that ended up being the greatest gift!

You see, in 2009 I had established a partnership with a colleague through which I brought her into one aspect of my business. On some level, in our second year of partnership, I knew everything wasn't fine… but I didn't *say* anything about it because that partnership was my only source of income at the time. It was the only sense of security I had which helped me sustain the difficult choice to file for bankruptcy.

But when she informed me that she wanted to dissolve the partnership, that was truly the "come to my knees" experience that burst my heart open! I felt emotions at a depth I never knew possible. Yes, some of those emotions were anger, hate, and rage, but there were also profound love, bliss, joy, and peace… unlike anything I'd ever felt before. I had no idea my emotions could be so deep and healing.

What I came to discover through this whole experience was that when everything was as "bad" as it had ever been in my life, I *was* really fine. How could that be? I sobbed for days. I was angry. I felt terrified. Yet I felt profound peace, witnessed countless miracles in my life, and was filled with gratitude.

I was grateful and peaceful because I could finally experience myself as being totally okay and totally fine in the midst of the most difficult and profound emotional experience I'd ever been through. Nothing was fine on the outside, but I truly was fine on the inside. I had finally found me! And that's what matters most.

I know it sounds crazy, but I assure you that when you allow your heart to open, and when you allow yourself to feel your emotions fully, share them with people you trust, and be okay even when everything on the outside is falling apart, your life will blossom in amazing ways. It's from your own emotional landscape that you're able to love deeply, be present with others, navigate any challenge that comes your way, and support loved ones when their hearts are hurting. These are the greatest gifts a person can ask for. This is when you can say "everything's fine" and truly mean it!

Christine Kloser, "The Transformation Catalyst," is a spiritual guide, award-winning author, and transformational book coach whose spot-on guidance transforms the lives of visionary entrepreneurs and authors around the world. Her passion is fueled by her own transformation in 2011 when she fully surrendered and discovered her authentic self. She now blends her passion for personal (and global) transformation with her gifts as a transformational book coach. Get her free training at www.ChristineKloser.com.

It All Starts with Me

Noni Boon

SEVEN YEARS AGO I ENROLLED IN A holistic counseling course on the premise that I had it ALL together and would be exceptional at dishing out advice and pinpointing what others needed to do in order to "fix" their lives. I was in for a rude shock and a large serving of humble pie! Little did I know I was going to slowly unravel and find myself vulnerable, exposed, and deeply contemplating my life. Within a short space of time, everything felt different. I was searching for answers and trying desperately to salvage the familiarity of my previous existence. By the end of the third year into my counseling course, I was separated from my husband of nineteen years, staring at divorce papers in disbelief, and pregnant with our miracle child.

When I was twenty years old, I married and became a mother in the same year. I had my second son at twenty-four, so I had very little time to focus on myself. My husband and I were busy trying to get ahead financially through renovating homes, moving a lot, and, at times, struggling to make ends meet. I studied graphic design and became a freelance designer while the boys were still young. I enjoyed my career and loved designing, learning new software, and running my own show. I excelled in my business and enjoyed the creative process along with the opportunity to work on high-end accounts and design marketing materials for some well-known brands.

Life chugged along pretty nicely and the boys were growing up fast. After many years as a freelance graphic designer, I decided to create something of my very own. I designed and created a café with a retail space that sold housewares from all over the world. Dealing with the public was a great experience for me and I learned a lot about people and being of service.

A few years later I sold the business and decided to take some time off. Before long I started to feel myself seeking more substance in my life. Something was stirring deep inside me, quietly whispering through my soft voice of intuition. I sensed that I was being called to do something more with my life. I wanted to help other people and make a difference in their lives, but first I had to help myself. I studied archetypes for six months and became an intuitive consultant, but still felt I needed more. I decided on holistic counseling.

I learned very early on in my counseling course that helping others was all about working on me. It had absolutely nothing to do with giving advice or directing other people's lives. In order to become a counselor, I had to explore every aspect of myself. I had to go deep and be truly open and honest. Like with any deep excavation, it uncovered dark places, stubborn issues, and unknown truths. It was hard going. I can remember times when I felt huge resistance. There were intervals when I maliciously disliked my teachers. "How dare they say THAT about me! They've got ME all wrong!" I'd think to myself. I was being protected by my ego defenses, and when they eventually came down I felt very insecure. It was a time of immense growth and it felt like I was being cracked open like a nut! Needless to say, this had a tremendous impact on my life, my marriage, and my family.

Holistic counseling is all about the whole person, how you live your life, the health of your spirit, your soul purpose, and your relationship to the existential. I launched into it in the same way that I dived into most things. I put my work boots on, rolled up my sleeves, and prepared to get sweaty and dirty. Living on a small farm and riding horses for sport, I was not afraid of hard work… and hard work it was. I questioned every aspect of myself, my life, my relationships, my grief, my unfinished business, my addictions, my ego, and particularly my shadow side. I started to clearly see areas of my life that were not working, not healthy, and in need of total renovation. The deep work on me had just begun and it wasn't going to be easy.

From a young age I had a fascination with self-help and spiritual books, and any words connected to good health, well-being, and personal growth. Although I had read many books that described all of the necessary tools required to create a better life and become a better person, no one had ever shown me how to use them and my life had not yet required it. They lay shiny and new, still in their packaging, in my library of resources. Thanks to my counseling course and the obvious need for personal growth, my relationship was put under the microscope and, of course, under immense pressure!

I pushed my husband away out of my sense of total frustration. I was irritated with myself, with my lack of self. I had been living my life by default and now I wanted to become a leader and design my life with consciousness and awareness. I wanted to lead myself and discover who I was outside of being a wife and mother. Being a graphic designer was not cutting it for me either. I wanted to self-actualize, reach my highest potential, and live a more empowered life. For some reason, I had to do the first six months of this on my own and in a deep state of grief, but God made sure I kept my connection to my husband. We had come to the conclusion that the past few years had been a struggle and that there had been more bad times than good. It looked like divorce was the only option for us.

The next week I found out that I was pregnant with our third child. I was thirty-nine years old and my two sons were fifteen and nineteen. While I grieved the end of my nineteen-year marriage and carried the relentless guilt for hurting my children, I also carried the constant reminder that my relationship had once thrived and could possibly thrive again. I just didn't know how to direct that change, how to make it all right. Instead, I prayed, I waited, and continued working on me.

It was not until we had been separated for nearly six months that the time was right and I had learned enough. We had divorce papers in front of us and had to make a final decision. By this stage I had totally let go of all expectation, all hope, and all neediness. I felt more aligned with God than ever before. Going to bed at night pregnant and alone after nineteen years of marriage was foreign to me. Every single night before I went to sleep, I prayed to God and felt warm in the knowing that I wasn't really alone and all would be well again. I grew a very strong spiritual connection during that time and I believe that is one of the main reasons why my life had to unfold in this manner.

After much soul searching and a lot of counseling, my husband and I decided not to get a divorce. Now, years later, I'm back in my marriage and I am a very different person from who I was before beginning my journey of self-growth and spiritual development. I have grown into my strength – into a larger, greater version of myself. I have more knowledge, more awareness, more patience, more compassion, more resilience, more endurance, and more stamina. These are many of the soul qualities that can only come about through struggle, hardship, and personal challenge. Now that these attributes are established in me, I can apply them in my life and help others develop the same strengths and beliefs in themselves and their abilities to be complete, fulfilled people both in and out of a relationship.

My focus has been on working on myself to transform my life. It's not about blaming anyone else for things that have gone wrong; it's about my taking responsibility, owning my shadow, and relaxing into the truth that I'm not perfect. When conflict comes about in my life now, the first questions I ask are: "What am I not seeing about myself? What are my ego defenses preventing me from owning?" and "How have I contributed to this situation?" I have learned that I can't control other people. I can't change them and I can't make them grow beyond their capacity. I can, however, control myself. I can remain conscious and aware. I can be the hero in my relationships and take charge when things are running off course.

What I take away from all of my experiences to date is the need to continually work on myself. It is a full-time job and everything else has to be slotted into the spaces that are left. My goal now is to have healthy, happy relationships with everybody in my life, strive to complete all of my unfinished business, let go of all resentments, and heal conflicts as quickly as possible. Living by this code is the only way to bring about inner peace and have a chance to create all of the wonderful things that I want in my life. Negative emotions lead to creative blocks that stop the flow of prosperity and sabotage the process of manifestation.

Life is like art. It needs to be created and designed upon a canvas of hope and dreams. Ideas and inspiration need to be brainstormed so that dreams can evolve and become concrete. I have learned that it is up to me to create the life I want, to dare to dream big, to have the courage to get out there and take a risk. When it comes to visualizing and working with the Law of Attraction, starting with a clean canvas is a creative necessity. A clean slate comes about through working on myself through self-examination, self-awareness, and self-love. I am a creative vessel and the clarity in which I co-create my life with God is a direct result of the amount of work I am prepared to do on myself. The results in my life show up when I clear myself of unwanted and unneeded creative, emotional, and archetypal blocks.

My warmblood horse, Suave, is one of my true teachers. He has taught me how to be a partner and how to be assertive without being controlling. He has taught me how to trust and then let go. He has shown me how to use my intuition and how to grow as a woman. At any moment he could hurt or even kill me, which has taught me respect and honor. Through show jumping, I have developed courage and learned how to control my fear. Through the subtleties of riding aids, I have discovered that the best results come about through learning what to do and how to do it, relaxing and releasing, taking and then giving. I have developed the stamina to get back in the saddle after some nasty falls and choose to look ahead. It is through the knowledge I absorbed in the classroom, the experiences I gained in life, and the relationships I have with my amazing husband, my incredible children, and my steadfast horse that I have evolved into the person I am today. For that I am most grateful and thankful. Most of all, I thank my greater self and the force that I call God for reaching out and calling me home.

I have now mastered each and every resource contained in my library of wisdom. I create my life in the same way that I create graphic design. I call upon the same principles, techniques, and rules that I apply to solve graphic design problems to help me with my life problems. I am now living an amazing life. It requires dedication and discipline to keep the slate clean and channel only the finest creative ideas into my life and relationships. I learned that visualizing and working with the Law of Attraction alone was not enough. In order to be a clean, clear, creative vessel, I needed to clear out the emotional blocks in my life that I didn't even know I had. I needed to work on myself, go deep, listen, and learn. My goal now is to share what I have learned through my studies and my life experiences with as many people as possible. This has made a tremendous difference in my life. I am now ready to launch my pebble and help others make a tremendous difference in theirs.

Noni Boon holds a diploma in arts, a certificate in holistic counseling, a certificate in communication skills, and is an accredited intuitive consultant. With her knowledge of art and life, Noni developed a series of five simple yet effective principles called "Life Design" that helps people find their creative power, channel clear inspiration, and completely transform their lives for the better. For more information about Noni's work, visit www.BiDesignCo.com or email her at Mail@BiDesignCo.com for a free half-hour consultation.

Intentional Transformation and Your Power to Be Free

MaryJo Briggs, MScEd

Obstacles, Opportunities, and Believing

IT WAS 2007, AND SEVERAL YEARS HAD PASSED since I'd been in rehab. My eating habits had improved, and my bulimic behaviors, when they involved food, were declining. Enjoying whole, unprocessed foods helped me nourish my inner knowing, access my intuition, and gain insight into my next step toward deeper healing. Yoga was helping me slow my mind and retrain my brain, taking the potential for a bulimic episode off the table. Instead of running straight to food for comfort, breath created a space for me to become present and aware of my immediate needs.

Life was good, but my world was small. I deeply desired to travel to experience new ways of being and wildly set my soul free. I knew this would nourish me more deeply and completely, but I'd never driven farther than three hours away from home. The idea of it made my head spin and my thoughts spiral out of control. Often after driving just thirty minutes I'd find myself paralyzed with anxiety and tears.

Something about driving got me thinking about the sexual and emotional abuse I'd been through and whether my family would ever believe me about it. After all, the man who had tainted the inner landscape of my mind, filling me with shame, pain, and secrecy, was not only a relative, he was a practicing priest in the Catholic faith. Forced to attend his ordination when I was a teen, the torment and the pain I felt filled me with fear. The drive to the church was dark, desolate, and debilitating. My once strong connection to Spirit or God seemed severed for life. A part of me died that day.

I deeply needed something that would nurture me and stop the downward spirals I found myself riding both before and after rehab. I didn't have a lot of money. In fact, I was bankrupt. I knew about the idea of asking for what I needed and then opening myself to receiving. With nothing to lose, I lovingly asked the Universe for a divine sign to inspire deeper healing.

Later that day while waiting to pay for groceries, I picked up a magazine. I thumbed through the pages and noticed a half-page ad with an invitation to an upcoming event – a completely free weekend at the Himalayan Institute. "Wow," I thought. "Miracles really do come true."

With my friends on standby as I made the six-hour drive, I pulled over many times to refocus and catch my breath. When I finally arrived at the Institute, my heart told me I was doing the right thing. I checked in, changed my clothes, and made my way to the meeting room. I knew I'd be required to remove my shoes because that was part of the ritual, and secretly my favorite part about yoga and meditation. But I became overwhelmed at the view outside this gathering space. Hundreds of pairs of shoes! They were everywhere. Some piled two feet high! "What have I gotten myself involved with?" I excitedly wondered.

I joyfully removed my flip-flops and went quietly inside. The workshop hadn't begun, but people were chanting and saying something repeatedly. I truly didn't know what to do. Then someone looked at me, touched my hand, and motioned for me to sit. After taking my place, I listened with intent and softly joined the chant. I had no idea what I was saying, but the vibration changed my energy and tiny tears ran down my face. As my chanting expanded and my voice seemed to break free, my body felt lighter.

The next day I woke in the sixteen-bed dormitory feeling a deep sense of peace, but also an undertone of anxiety. I sat on my top bunk, hunched over the beads I'd brought to distract me from any sort of eating disorder behavior. Too anxious to make the six-hour drive home but too scared to leave my beads for fear I'd run to food, I was terrified and deeply distraught.

A woman entered the room. She'd forgotten something and asked if I was okay. I gently said, "Not really." I told her I had become addicted to beading since trying to put my eating disorder to rest. We talked for a while, and then she took the necklace from around her neck. It was something I'd rarely seen: an elephant head on a chain. "Ganesha is his name. He's the God of Wisdom and remover of all obstacles. Wear it until we leave, please." I could tell she really believed in what she was saying. I wanted to believe, too, so I put the necklace around my neck and together we returned to the workshop.

I never did know her name. At the end of the weekend I searched for her to give her necklace back, but I couldn't find her. When it came time to leave, I wrapped Ganesha up in an organza bag I had for my own beads, wrote a little thank-you note, and placed it on her bed.

My drive home was peaceful, pleasant, and uneventful. When I returned to my beading, I did so with intention instead of addiction. Worshiped as the God of education, knowledge, wisdom, and success,

Ganesha, the Hindu elephant deity, has had a profound impact on my life. A small statue of him now sits before me and assists in times of need. Ganesha helped me realize that all the answers I need reside inside of me. His presence creates a space for release. Yoga, chanting, and the heartfelt acts of kindness I experienced during that weekend at the Institute freed me to more deeply believe in me.

Intention, Divine Guidance, and Believing in Things Unseen

It was July of 2011, eighteen months after the car accident. I was home, in bed, getting ready to start my day. I kept agonizing over not wanting to see my neurologist. Diagnosed with something called post concussive syndrome, I experienced debilitating dizziness and massive migraines, and further testing showed a mild traumatic brain injury leaving me in constant pain and anguish.

I recalled that I had secretly wanted to attend a workshop being held that day at Lily Dale Assembly called "To Touch the Soul." I knew I needed deeper healing. Something about the car accident unearthed past issues of abuse and victimization, and decades of repressed emotion and fear faced me head on. I thought I'd processed all this stuff, but instead I found my life beginning to spiral out of control again. I thought that perhaps if my soul was touched it would speed my healing. Was it possible that this accident was part of some grander plan? Could it be an opportunity to nourish myself more deeply, transforming the cells of my body and the inner landscape of my mind? This was something I secretly desired to do, but didn't completely know how or where to begin. Regardless, I remained in my bed, confused in the midst of my pain.

I wasn't sure what choice to make – drive forty-five miles to see my doctor or go to Lily Dale Assembly. So I did what I always do. I sat on the edge of my bed and set my simple intention for the day, then gently placed my feet on the floor to begin my day.

"My intention is to heal more deeply," I whispered. Immediately my heart spoke and had me dressed and driving to the Dale in fifteen minutes! I was five minutes late and there was just one chair left. Once seated, I reviewed the outline for the week and knew it was impossible to ignore the depth of what I had signed up for.

"To Touch the Soul – On Becoming a Medium"! What had I gotten myself into? I thought at first to ask for my $350 dollars back. The experiences of that workshop were so indescribably wonderful that I can't begin to recount them in this space. I will say that I began my mediumship on the very first day. Opening myself up to allow Spirit to speak to and through me allowed for deeper healing and the divine guidance I so desired. It was magical, mystical, and healing for all involved.

What happened after the event was even more profound. Double dolphins, Buddha, little brown lodges, a rustic old cafeteria, and a beautiful purple bedroom kept reappearing in my dreams, though I had no idea why these became a recurring theme. Three months later when I found my way to Delphi University to attend the Arthur Ford International Academy of Mediumship, I could hardly believe my eyes!

The University was situated atop a copper-filled mountain consisting of little brown lodges. Life-sized statues of two double dolphins and a chubby Buddha greeted me at the entrance to the gift shop. Back at the dormitory I found the beautiful purple bedroom and the rustic cafeteria exactly as they appeared in my dreams! My dreams had definitely come true!

One small intention, simply recited as I sat in pain on the edge of my bed, had changed the entire course of my life, helping me heal more deeply. It opened a channel for me to provide divine guidance to those in need and to help you and others believe in things unseen.

Food, Fear, and the Real Meaning of Bulimia

It was July of 2012, and I had a workshop of my own to write. "The Spirituality of Food" was the topic. The entire outline of the workshop was channeled to me from Spirit the summer before I even knew what channeling was. I loved giving presentations, but since the brain injury I had struggled with putting things together in a logical, linear way. "Why did I sign up to give this talk?" I wondered.

I had no idea how to begin. In my bulimic days I'd simply run to food to calm my fears, and eventually purge to give me that boost of endorphins I deeply needed to proceed. But with those days over I needed to find a new way. I gathered information and tried putting it together. That didn't work, and besides, I wasn't even sure what I was supposed to be writing about. The harder I tried to logically organize and linearly create my workshop, the more impossible the task became. I was hugely confused.

I looked at the outline over and over again. My heart told me I was being divinely guided to share how I had overcome many life obstacles, not just my bulimia and emotional eating. But I lacked clear insight into how I achieved true prosperity, deep healing, and peace.

So once again I lay in bed ready to set my intention for the day. I let my heart speak. "I intend to allow Spirit to show me how to begin creating my presentation." And by the time my toes touched the floor I saw a pyramid. Intrigued, I hurried to my computer and learned some fascinating bits of ancient information. As I explored the secrets of the Great Pyramid, I discovered the golden ratio, a symbol of balance and harmony between moderation and excess. This ratio is present through all of nature. As I dug deeper I found the spiral of nourishment, which, like the pyramids, is based on the golden ratio. Uncovering this information helped me realize that the very things I was doing to improve my health and life circumstances nourished my inner knowing, making it simpler to overcome life obstacles and helping me set my soul free!

The secret of the spiral lies in the ratio of what we need to consume to create health and vitality. Two key ingredients in the spiral, which mainstream medicine seldom mentions, are air and water. Breath establishes life, and without it life ends. You can only go a few minutes without breath and not more than a day or two without water.

Focused, intentional breathing and plentiful, pure water made it easier for me to reprogram my mind, release limiting beliefs, manage my pain, and choose to consume things that truly nourished me on all levels: physical, emotional, spiritual, relational, and mental.

What I ate mattered. Eating organic, clean foods 90 percent of the time helped me transform my mind and body, igniting my intuition quickly. Why I had eaten with reckless abandon was more difficult to figure out, but obviously not impossible. I viewed my recovery as a process, not an event. A journey to allow myself to be free!

As I look back, I realize that bulimia was a set of beliefs and behaviors that kept me from experiencing my divine gifts. It provided me with only temporary relief in times of desperate need. Spirit led me to a new definition of B.U.L.I.M.I.A.: Beliefs and Behaviors Undermining Living an Illuminated, Inspirational, Magnetic and Intentional life in Alignment with your truest desires.

I truly want to inspire you to create a life of your own divine design no matter what your life challenge or circumstance. Here are some simple, but not easy, things you can begin to do now to find your way:

First, do not let your problems define you. This will only keep you stuck. Instead, step back for a wider perspective that will allow you to become aware of the vast array of opportunities that every challenging behavior or situation presents.

Second, begin expressing gratitude for something or someone regularly. This will enhance your connection to God or the Universal Source.

Next, begin setting intentions daily. As you can see from my story, they are powerful beyond belief.

Fourth, explore organic and whole-food options. Choose foods that contain five ingredients or fewer, and if you can't pronounce an ingredient, select something different.

Fifth, listen to your heart. It knows your truest desires and rarely leads you astray.

Sixth, ask for divine guidance. It is always available to you, but you must ask specifically for what you need.

Next, begin a yoga or meditation practice. This is key to elevating your awareness and creating sustained change.

And last but not least, in times of greatest need, breathe mindfully and allow your body to feel, knowing that your mind is free to rest within the breath. Using breath as a tool to train your mind helps stop any downward spirals you may find yourself in. More important, breath helps you cope, heal, and find lasting comfort and peace, allowing you to move forward and create a life beyond your wildest dreams!

Regarding the details of how I created the rest of my presentation, "The Spirituality of Food"– all of it was channeled to and through me, and I divinely presented the workshop, which was an incredible success!

MaryJo Briggs, MScEd, AADP, is a spiritual guide, psychic intuitive, registered medium, and gifted transformational writer. She empowers women globally to create passionate, purposeful lives free from the struggles of addiction, victimization, and chronic disease. Known for her ability to inspire women to transcend limiting beliefs, her new books, *Windows of Awareness: A Mystics Guide to Bulimia-Free Living* and *The Spirituality of Food* release in 2013. Receive MaryJo's free training, "The 7 Steps to Mastering the Energy of Intention" at www.MaryJoBriggs.com.

The Two Yous:
How and Why to Awaken to
Your Soul

Janis Fossette Butler, BA

ONE DAY WHEN I WAS IN THE SIXTH GRADE I was walking to school alone. The sun was streaming down through the cool California coastal morning haze. I raised my eyes to follow the Jacob's Ladders – columns of sunlit rays – through a gap in the clouds to their source, and I thought of the Sunday school hymn "We Are Climbing Jacob's Ladder." Retracing the rays to the ground, I watched myself sniff small, spicy-sweet carnations next to the sidewalk. I looked at myself in my school clothes, my arms and legs rhythmically alternating places, saddle oxfords appearing, disappearing out of my vision. *"What's this about?"* I went around for days watching *me*. How could there be two of me? I wondered if I'd gone weird. Gradually I settled into acceptance of the other me appearing at times. I had become aware of the Observer, my watching consciousness, the way-shower to my Soul, my Authentic Self. I was present. This was no out-of-body experience. I was simply, literally out of my mind.

The Two of Me

I am now in the "mature years," no longer living as I did when young – unconsciously reacting to life rather than actively creating it. In my earlier years, I hadn't the tools to maintain awareness apart from my mind. However, Spirit kept nudging me into my "Observer Self," offering occasional awakenings until I learned to pay attention. Through more experiences I could move easily into presence with myself, with my Soul, and with Spirit, living from my heart rather than my head. Today I know how to tune in to Spirit's guidance when it comes. I call these occurrences "knowings."

I don't hear voices other than my own, nor do I have special psychic sight. I merely experience clear, memorable knowings, sometimes as vibrations of energy coursing through my body, and occasionally in meditation or when my mind has shifted into a lower gear. I bet you do, too. If you aren't sure, begin paying attention to your gut or wherever your intuition surfaces, including your mind, and whenever these promptings show up.

For me, an "aha!" moment can come out of nowhere. For example, after teaching language arts to elementary school students, I was fortunate to be a stay-at-home mom and volunteer worker until Emily, my youngest, was in eighth grade. One evening, legs tucked under me on the carpet at a social gathering, I was listening to a teacher mention a summer program for Spanish teachers. Instantly my Soul tapped me, and I *knew* I needed to pursue this.

I'd never been in a Spanish classroom, although I did know some Spanish. Nonetheless, I quickly took classes over the next year-and-a-half, achieving a degree in Spanish in addition to my earlier BA and teaching certificate. I taught the language for eight years. When I receive a strong knowing, I am compelled to act no matter the strangeness of it. If not, I suffer. And when I follow through, the end result is always good and right.

Self-Reflection Allows for Perspective

You and I have the ability to be self-aware: to feel, to think, to search for meaning, to be self-reflective. When you notice that what bothers another doesn't touch you in the same way, you realize it's each person's own perceptions that govern his or her responses to what's happening. What and how we absorb is an inside job. Growing up at home with my older brother John, I was lonely a lot. John wasn't. So my interpretations of goings-on were different from his, as were my needs — we each had our own subjective view of things. If I'd had some distance from my experiences, I might not have had the same reactions. I wasn't awake to my spiritual nature.

In Hurting, There's an Opening

Often in suffering or times when you feel down, you go into questioning, wanting to make changes. Through introspection you uncover a longing for something else… something more. Sometimes you can't even define it — this yearning. Thus begins or intensifies your seeking spiritual awareness. Your Authentic Self, your Soul, evolves naturally, uniquely, in its own time and manner. We all awaken — really, it's a remembering — to our true nature as a Soul having a human experience. It's simply a matter of when.

Skidding to the floor in disarray or despair may be your unhappy impetus to opening to your loving Presence within. I have always been spiritually inclined. However, it was in the aftermath of my second husband's long-term affair that I dragged myself up enough times to turn pursuits of the Soul into my passion.

You see, I *knew* the first week he began with his mistress, but I wasn't going to be divorced twice. I had successfully brought our blended family together through our twenty years of marriage. I hung in, shoving my Soul's wisdom down deep, refusing to acknowledge completely what Spirit kept presenting.

Holding on to my husband wasn't worth what I put myself through. With cobwebs for brains, my energy drained into the gutter. I existed in confusion, desperately depressed. *I betrayed myself, which cost me greatly.*

The Observing You

What we think about expands. What I was holding in my mind could have undone me.

Once on my own in a new city, I actively searched for that Observer Self that had been surfacing involuntarily since childhood. *There,* in the observer-witness mode, was space. *There* was freedom from my overactive mind — when this Presence and my Soul were present. *There* was calm.

I would soften my focus, taking my awareness out into the room. Try this exercise with me now:

First be in your body exclusively, just you and this page. Got it? Now let your attention move into the space around you while still continuing to read. Can you project your consciousness from that wider vantage point back to where you are sitting reading this? Kind of like it's another person, huh? Your senses are still with you as you read, but with this added "walleyed" vision, thoughts slow and almost seem like someone else's. They are. You are not your thoughts, or feelings, or moods, or tiredness. You are Soul.

Once I grabbed hold of this part of me – this other perspective – I could choose again. If I found myself in a low mental state, I could choose another – when I remembered to stand back in my Observer Self. I was in charge and responsible for myself. Events didn't rule. From this expanded observer-witness viewpoint, another aspect of consciousness is available. By softening and enlarging your attention, you can notice your thoughts without judging them, thereby disempowering your mind, however briefly, so your Soul can come forth. A mere moment in your silence is relief and distance from the issues of your mind.

Even though observing occurs occasionally unbidden, once you practice inviting it to come forth consciously, you might wonder as I did where your observer state comes from. Observing and witnessing is a trait of your consciousness, separate from your mind, your personality, your ego – as is your awareness. And this impersonal awareness is part of the universal field of consciousness... namely God. If God is everywhere and always present, then your consciousness is an aspect of God's loving Presence. There's loving goodness inside of you. Your Observer-Witness Self is the "open sesame" to your Soul and to your Spirit – God in you.

Why Connect with Your Soul?

Yes, why? Because your Soul is the core of who you are – your True Self – whose nature is unconditional love. This is *you*. What could be more amazingly wonderful? Through self-understanding, a wider perspective of your life is possible. You can consider your Soul's purpose apart from your ego and your personality's goals and drives. You can consider that unsettling experiences are opportunities for your Soul's learning, which can take the "ouch" out of them. You can consider that your Soul wants to grow in love and wisdom, and that love and compassion to yourself and others can be your responses to challenges in your life.

In an audio series called *The Discovery: Revealing the Presence of God in Your Life,* Dr. David Hawkins said that "Spirituality is a way of being in the world." Not doing; being. Being loving, grateful, compassionate. Perhaps you have heard this advice: When you have a choice between being kind and being right, choose kindness. This is your Higher Self graciously responding. Allow it.

It is only in the present that I can be with my Soul, whom I call Sophia in order to bring her into my focused awareness. When I am meditating or in the observer role, I find this very moment more easily. Here I can process events instead of getting caught up in the story. Here is where intuition and creativity bloom. I can trust and turn things over to Sophia, my conduit to the Divine. Here, right now, is when spiritual awakenings come; when I *know* from experience what I've read and heard about.

Finding Your Soul – The Other You

After I started anew, fresh – or rather wilted – from divorce, I was still dealing with depleted adrenals and mental fatigue. I had always walked my dogs, so I began including walking meditations. As a way to help me move into a flow, I would locate my Observer first. You might like to play with this exercise on your next walk or hike:

On a bright day, grab your sunglasses and walk with the sun to your back or at your side. Notice your shadow. Do this for a while.

Then look at the rim of your shades. From there, catch a glimpse of your arm coming in and out of your vision. Move your gaze farther out to a tree or a building while maintaining awareness of yourself. If you are thinking at all, you have greatly reduced your thoughts per second.

Keep practicing this perspective as often as you remember to do so. You'll find the observer role calming as well as intriguing. *"There I am. Hi! I've found me again."*

The Protector

We had Petunia for only a summer. Half Brittany, half Labrador, Petunia was a black, fur-ball, fun-loving puppy. Daisy, "The-Family-Dog," as Emily had named her, was a great nanny, training Petunia in the house rules and family ways. The hardest for Petunia was "Thou shalt not follow strangers." On a family hike in the mountains, one minute Petunia was there by Daisy, the next gone, trailing after other hikers for half an hour until we located her.

By the start of Emily's senior year, Petunia, now four months old, had mastered "doing her dos" outside. One night Daisy came in without her. A couple of Emily's guy friends were coming up the walk as we opened the front door to call for Petunia. They told us they'd seen a pack of dogs crossing busy MacArthur Street. Petunia must have seen them running through our neighborhood and taken off after them. She was dead when my husband got to her crumpled body on the street. *"She was just outside a couple of minutes. It's not so! Bring her back! I'm sorry, Petunia!"* About to be overwhelmed by grief and blame, I found myself in witness mode, observing myself wailing, racing around the house grabbing up Petunia's toys, her bed, her bowls, throwing them in a box in the garage. My Observer was shielding me from becoming engulfed by the tragedy until I could cope.

After Petunia's accident, my feelings collapsed into stunned retreat, allowing me to slowly absorb Petunia's death. My Soul tended to me and my Observer buffered me. Yours can protect you as well from the unpredictable whims and stresses of your feelings and thoughts. Your Observer will remind you that no matter what's going on, the core of you is not touched.

The Worth of Awakening

Your Soul will love and expand with your recognition of it and will offer opportunities to know it better. Watch for them. Your Soul has an insightful voice. How do you know who's talking? It could be the many voices of your mind, couldn't it? Direct from God, your Soul is positive, supportive, affirming, and uncritical of you or anyone. After all, we are all blessed little Souls having a human experience, even that jerk down the block. When I see myself and others with Soul-centered eyes, I cannot help but notice everyone's loving Presence. And guess what? Bit by bit those other misguided persons soften and sweeten up. Really. I've tried it. It works. This is what is meant by the precious Hindu greeting *namaste,* with hands before heart in prayer position: the divine loving Light in me bows to the divine loving Light in you. We are one.

A plus of my having life-long recurrences of loneliness is that I find that with awakenings I don't go into lonely much – now that I am aware of Sophia and Spirit. I have company and so do you – loving beings like Sophia, and angels, and guides with whom to commune. And they love and need to be asked to help. They won't help unless you ask. It's against spiritual laws.

What's the worth of becoming acquainted with the True You? More contentment, more belonging, more perspective, more relief from mind, more smiling, and more direction for your life straight from

Source, your friend, your Soul. This is what I want for you. Please let me know how this exploration progresses!

Take care and be happy.

Janis Butler received a BA in history with a minor in French from Stanford University. She received a post bachelor's credential in elementary language arts. Later she received a BA in Spanish and taught Spanish for eight years. She is currently pursuing a master's degree in spiritual psychology at the University of Santa Monica and writing *THE TWO YOUS: How to Awaken to Your Soul and Be Present to Yourself and to Life*. Visit www.JanisFossetteButler.com for more information.

Journey of Self to Soul

Tara Chatterton

WOW! WHAT AN AMAZING JOURNEY I've been on so far! Where do I begin? Thinking back to my younger years, to the person I was and the lessons that I've learned since then, I couldn't say I would change any of my experiences... not a single second of them. They were the building blocks I had to discover in order to become the person I am today.

Funny enough, after all is said and done, I'm grateful that I've made it this far in life. The distant and difficult childhood I lived led to my wayward teenage years, which, of course, progressed to my out-of-control early twenties. Included in this mix were a major car accident and the years of healing afterward both mentally and physically. To say the least, it's been interesting. Through all these ordeals I was also dealing with alcohol and substance abuse and all that goes with that, including constant bouts of depression.

At the age of twenty-two-and-a-half, I spiraled into the worst depression I'd ever experienced. It was the first in which I had been so debilitated. But they say you sometimes have to hit rock bottom in order to choose whether to give up or get back up and try again. I am forever grateful that I chose to crawl back from the darkness, even though I knew that the things I had been struggling with weren't working in my life anymore.

I started to make changes in my life, taking small steps in the beginning. I began to listen to my intuition, which I knew had always been strong — I had just chosen not to acknowledge it when it didn't suit me. I started to listen to my gut instinct, for which I'm very glad. It led me to the beginning of my insight, which ignited the next part of my journey.

It was around this time in my life that I was drawn to a sense of knowing that I would have a baby boy named Jackson at the age of twenty-four. I researched how to do a holistic detoxification of my body and mind in order to prepare for this special event, and sure enough, when I was twenty-four, I gave birth to my angel, Jackson. This was a soul-changing event for me beyond words.

My life continued to be interesting, as the more I followed my heart and intuition, the better my life became. In doing this, I gained enough courage to leave the five-year relationship I was in, and I became a single mother of six-month-old baby Jackson. At the time, this decision ranked high on my difficulty list, as it was one of the toughest things I'd ever done. The fear I had was mind-boggling. I remembered that a wise woman once said to me, "Happy mother, happy child," and at the time that was all that mattered.

In hindsight, I couldn't agree more with the choices I made back then as my intuition began to play a major role in my life. Every day I was healing and growing with my newfound independence, eventually becoming the me I was always meant to be. I was able to break away from my old addictions and habits, and truly unlock and find my true self. Things seemed as if they were just falling into place for me, so much so that I even remember saying on quite a few occasions to my friends, "I feel like I'm starring in a movie!" I guess you could call this awakening of myself *divine intervention at its best*.

It was while going through this process of healing, which involved releasing my emotions, accepting that everything happens for a reason, and learning to love myself again, that I came discover that I had many talents. They had been lying dormant in my soul and were just itching to be brought to the surface. My writing, for example, is what helps me express my gifts. It's amazing just how powerful the written word can be and how much of an impact it can have on us. It's also given me the opportunity to tell my story, and for that reason alone I feel blessed.

It was shortly after embarking on my journey to find myself that I unlocked a voice from within that still surprises me sometimes. I had always known that I could sing, even throughout my troubled years. I had been drawn to different types of music on my journey, and found it to be soothing. It just took a few life lessons and some confidence boosting before I was ready to unlock this talent within me.

I also noticed a strong pull towards yoga. Things presented themselves all around me that highlighted the practice of yoga, and when it comes to following my intuition, I look for such clear signs. Yoga seemed to appear everywhere I looked, from books I happened to see, to conversations I had and people I met, whether they were teachers of yoga or practiced it daily; and the list goes on. It's all about learning to acknowledge the synchronicity of events as they happen, no matter how big or small. I had a strong feeling that yoga constantly showing up for me meant something, but it didn't go any further at the time; I had other priorities to settle. But if I had known what was to unfold in the coming months, I would have paid more attention to this message.

I had managed to set up myself and Jackson comfortably in our new surroundings, and had finally tied up all the loose ends from my past. By focusing on myself and healing from the inside out, even though only a year had passed, I had come a long way. I was now a strong, independent woman, and had unlocked my true self, and in doing so I felt the eternal happiness of my soul. Although at times I battled with some of the hardest decisions and situations I've ever had to face, I kept trying my utmost to live in the now, follow my intuition, and go with the flow of events of my life.

Somehow in my map of synchronistic events I managed to stumble across the opportunity to attend a weekend healing workshop based on the ancient practice of *sat nam rasayan*. At the time, to be honest, I didn't have much of an idea of what it was all about; I was just looking at all opportunities that presented themselves as positive experiences, and thought, "What do I have to lose if I attend this workshop?" I also believed that I could perhaps learn something new to incorporate into my new lifestyle, and learn I did.

Sat nam rasayan means "deep relaxation into your true self." It is an ancient healing form based on the principles of healing through silence in a meditative and sometimes transcendent state, and through boundless consciousness. The transcendent state is achieved through total meditative absorption between the healer and client. The healer goes through a process of stabilizing and enters into a very high state of awareness, increasing their sensitivity. Once this state is reached, congestions and imbalances in the client are released and healing takes place. This brings a deep state of peace and bliss to the healer as well as the client as the healer enters a very high meditative state and vast consciousness. The one word I would choose to describe this practice is *amazing*. I now have a new "addiction" per se, and it's not harmful to myself or others. It's actually beneficial.

Sat nam rasayan is unique to the healing traditions of kundalini yoga, which I have also started to practice. The two practices combined have helped me heal even further, and they have definitely improved my physical, mental, and spiritual development, providing me with strength to live my everyday life.

Today nothing makes me smile more than knowing that I have made the right decision for my both myself and Jackson. He now has a healthy and happy mum and a positive role model in his life, which is more than I could ask for.

This brings me to the present moment in my quest to live in the now. I can honestly say that I wouldn't change anything I've had to endure in my lifetime – not a single second of it. Instead of letting these events break me, I have chosen to let them shape me. Everything is and will be perfect in the end; you just have to learn to go with the flow, as you are the bearer of your own happiness.

I will leave you at the end of this leg of my journey. Only time will truly tell what's around the corner for me, but now I realize that everything I need, I already have within me – it's what I choose to do with it that counts. This will surely make for a continued interesting life.

Peace and light to you on your own journey.

Tara Chatterton healed herself from emotional and physical wounds and now enjoys encouraging others to heal and reach their full potential. She continues her learning, understanding, and practice of *sat nam rasayan*, the ancient healing art in the tradition of kundalini yoga. Along with her love of wisdom and music, she makes time for writing, singing, and more important, the growth of her son. You can contact her at tara.chatterton1@gmail.com and https://twitter. com/@TaraChatterton.

The Art of Becoming a Magnet for Transformation

Bo Eason

WHEN I WAS NINE, I DRAFTED A TWENTY-YEAR plan and at the end of that plan I would be the best safety in the NFL. I drew it up with crayons I stole from my sister and constructed it out of school paper. And at the end of those twenty years, that dream and that plan actually came true. I had become the best safety in the NFL and so I got to live that dream... for four seasons. Then surgery #7 on my knee forced me to reevaluate that twenty-year plan.

I knew I needed to channel all the massive amount of pent-up energy I had into something constructive or I'd likely end up in jail or worse. I had to undergo a personal transformation and uncover what I was supposed to do with the rest of my life. Football was not an option anymore. All those years of hard work, of clawing my way up the ladder to playing professional football with the Houston Oilers were now behind me. And like most people when facing a shift in consciousness, my first question was "Now what?"

While I was at college, I'd sneak over to the drama department and take classes, but none of my teammates ever knew about my desire to be an actor. And then when I became a professional player, I would

45

take acting classes during the off-season, but again, I never let my teammates know because I just didn't want to get teased about it. So after my football career was completely finished, I moved to New York City and started studying acting full time. I discovered that I also liked to write and an idea began to germinate in my brain. What if I wrote about my own story? What if I could share some of my own enthusiasm and dedication for achieving goals with an audience? What if I could connect with other human beings and inspire them to go out and do what they were truly meant to be?

From that thought, my speaking career and subsequent play *Runt of the Litter* was born.

I remember when the play first opened in New York and I was doing an interview with the *New York Times*. The reporter had finished writing a sentence after I said something when he turned to me and said, "You know, that's a sentence that's never been uttered. NFL player turned Broadway playwright. I've never written that sentence before." I said, "Yeah, and it's probably never going to happen again." It's totally seemed the most unlikely of paths, but for me it was the absolute right direction to take.

A lot of people come up to me after I've done a speaking presentation or have put on the play and they say, "I want to be magnetic like you are on stage. But Bo, I don't have a good story like you've got." And I say, "That's bull. That's a cop-out. The reason why I'm more magnetic on stage than you right now is because you haven't made the decision yet. And the decision is this: I love my story more than you love your story. And there's nothing I won't do onstage to inspire you. That's the main difference between us." I call this the power of magnetism. It's a decision and a commitment that you have to make as a performer, as a speaker, as an author – in any aspect of your chosen path to step up and stand out.

No matter what your chosen career path may be, you have to perform. You have to bring yourself forth and lay your heart and your blood on a blank page. My favorite definition for the word magnetism is: he has the power to affect others with the delight he takes in himself. So it doesn't matter if you're the best performer, the best writer, the best singer, or even the best athlete. It doesn't matter if you don't have the best story. What matters is that you love the story more than everyone else loves their story. That's what's key.

And as soon as you start telling that one person and connecting to them, once your message has "landed" then they have to reciprocate. You have to wait for it to come back, the energy that is. Then as soon as that happens, you move to the next person. You connect, you make it land, the energy comes back to you, and then you move to the next person. Because when you're writing a book, giving a presentation, or performing on stage, if you try to please them all in one shot, it's going to be too general. It's going to be too unspecific and blurry. Your energy and message has got to land on one person at a time to be most magnetic and transformational.

If you notice, the people who are the most magnetic, the greatest performers, whether it's Mikhail Baryshnikov, Al Pacino, a saxophone player, or an author, they're magnetic because you know they love what they do. They fall in love with their own lot in life. They surrender to their own work. And I'm not saying that that work isn't without pain because most great art comes from pain, but as great artists, we surrender to that pain and we say, "I love my story and my work more than anyone else."

A huge part of capturing your audience's attention (whether it be 1 person or 1,000 people) and keeping it is to constantly focus on them. I always look people straight in the eye and deliver my message directly to that person. I don't want people to rustle their jacket or rummage through their purse for a piece of gum during my onstage performances. With my eyes I send them a message saying, "Don't move. This is important information that I'm about to deliver to you." I was taught this technique by Jean-Louis Rodrigue who dedicated his life to observing the movement and habits of animals.

If you have that intent, no one will move. No one will take their eyes off you because they don't know they're afraid. They just know that they have to be aware because they're dealing with something that's alive onstage in front of them. I'm telling you, if you capture that feeling when speaking or writing about your own story, people will feel compelled by you. They want more of you... because you're mesmerizing. It's called love at first sight. It's sexual attraction. It's what we all feel as humans every day when somebody walks by and we go, "Wow. Why am I attracted to them? Why do I stare at them?" It's because something in them is alive and is close to their true nature.

The person who can transform others — using the power of their story — the most or the best is the "winner," — the one who will impact the most lives. That seems kind of magical and many of you may wonder how do we put our arms around transforming other people? I'll tell you, it's very simple. To transform others you have to transform yourself right in front of them, while giving them permission and the enlightenment to transform themselves. And by doing this, you're going to transform yourself and they'll transform right along with you.

The best way for you to transform yourself is to share your personal story because no story in itself has ever been told that didn't involve someone going through a transformation. That's why every great movie, every great book, every great story starts at the bottom of a person's climb to authenticity.

Every one of us has this transformational story inside of us. And we have to share that to distinguish ourselves from everyone else because it's our biggest calling card. In fact, I would argue that your specific personal story is your biggest money maker, and is the biggest influence that you can have on the world.

If myself and the futurists are right about this story-telling age and how the iconic figure is going to be the one who can impact people emotionally, whether their product is physical or not, then everyone has to tell their story. If you have the ability to impact people emotionally, through your own story, then you're the iconic leader. So, the best way to access all that phenomenal power is for you to go back to that lowest moment when it looked like there were no answers and you start there (just like you're reading about in many of the chapters in this book).

Usually there was a decision made right after that event happened where you either said, "Okay, I quit. I will not participate with humanity anymore," or you decided to fight because your message was more important than the way you felt. You moved forward. That story started at your lowest point and it ends with where you are on the other side of that transformation.

You see, vulnerability is the new power. People used to seek power by seeking external power over others. No longer. It doesn't work in today's world. What's powerful is vulnerability. What makes you vulnerable is sharing your authentic self. You've got to let go of the control. Most of us — when we're in front of people and sharing our true selves — want to control how people view us. Well, it's time to give that up.

If you're willing to give all you have and be vulnerable, people won't be able to turn away. It goes right back to the magnetism I was talking about. That's why when somebody accidentally gets vulnerable, such as when they are being interviewed on *Oprah* or even the news, it captures our attention. At first they come across as being very strong in stating their truth, when all of sudden if the interviewer asks them about their mom, their voice suddenly cracks. Anyone watching thinks, "Whoa. What just happened?" And you can't take your eyes off them as the person shared with you a *real* moment. If you put your story out there, then you've got to make yourself vulnerable. You've got to show and share your pain... and your transformation.

I'm telling you that there's a universe out there that is invisible to you right now that will be revealed to you... if you have the bravery and the courage to share your personal self every day, all the time, and be vulnerable in the moment. If you have the ability to do that, then you must do it. There's a finite number of us out here who are willing to be so vulnerable. But you've probably heard the saying that sometimes people need a story, or need a word, more than they need food to survive. It's true – and your story can make that difference to another.

Bo Eason ~ Former NFL standout, acclaimed Broadway playwright, performer, and Presence/Story Coach to some of the most successful people in the world. His play, *Runt of the Litter*, written and performed by Bo, has toured over fifty cities nationally. The New York Times named it, "One of the most powerful plays in the last decade." Soon to be a major motion picture, Bo is adapting *Runt* for the big screen. He is co-founder of World's Greatest Speaker Training with Brendon Burchard, and a Senior Fellow with CEG Worldwide where he is the co-founder of Perfecting Your Personal Story and Power of Presence. Bo Eason's Personal Story Power Programs have reinvented how speakers communicate. www.BoEason.com

ChristIAm,
Who We Are in Truth

Marilyn Garrett

"Yes, ChristIAm, take on that name before the conscious self feels the journey is complete…. You are the Christ. You cannot be someone or something else until you achieve the goal – the Christ. You are always, you have always been, you always will be the Christ. You cannot be any-one else but the Christ, as are all of My Beloved. *Accept the challenge of who you are, and knowing who you are, make the journey. … slip and fall if you must, but do so knowing who you are…. The name is who you are – ChristIAm."* – Spoken by Spirit God, March 19, 1989.

WHAT IS YOUR FIRST REACTION TO READING this challenge? It is actually OUR challenge, not just mine. WE are always, WE cannot be anyone else but the Christ – the name is who YOU are – ChristIAm! What follows is my chapter of our story, the journey as ChristIAm.

"When others of My Beloved touch this moment in days to come, by read-ing the written record of it, they will derive as their greatest truth a mir-

ror of themselves as a Spiritual being. And the Christ within them shall stir the conscious self to open to their truth, to listen for the voice within, and to become seekers of that truth and of the treasures."

— Spoken by Spirit God, March 20, 1989.

My story begins where spiritual journeys often do. When ordinary days of our lives hit a brick wall, when failure seems certain, when crises are overpowering, it seems there is no hope, no clear path ahead. When we are ready to give up, that's when we are finally willing to ask the big questions such as: What is the purpose of my life? What is success? Does God exist? Am I being punished? Why me?

The personal crises that led me to this state of mind and outer condition are not important. It is more pertinent that my crises mirrored those of others — as individuals, as nations, and as a world. Crisis conditions exist for more people than ever in our lifetime, and our collective state of mind seems desperate, ready to ask the big questions and look for new truths. Thus these may not be the worst of times; they may indeed be the best of times for transforming human consciousness!

Let's get on with my story. Though my body was caving in from stress, I did not sink into depression, because as a single parent, failure was not an option. Nor did I fall for the temporary escape offered by drugs and alcohol. Without health insurance, I also did not rush to a doctor hoping for a "cure," a magic pill, or at least sympathy and an excuse for failing. Fortunately I was led instead to self-help, guided imagery, and meditation. The peaceful environment at Orlando's Spiral Circle Metaphysical Bookstore reduced the stress, and owner Beverly Ford, famous for soulful hugs, offered loving support!

Following a really bad day, I aroused from meditation surprised to find a message written in the journal I kept beside me. It was my first experience of receiving dictation from God's voice within!

"Beloved, it is I, Spirit. I know thou art weary of many trials. But concentrate on the beauty of sight and sound, and act only on the positive path to the Spirit you are within... Let your footsteps etch the path of Spirit on earth as you journey through the day, knowing, feeling only the joy and peace and love of the Oneness of your being and the living Christ. Come Beloved, rest, and waken with a glad heart."— Spoken by Spirit God, January 9, 1989.

Startling as this was, nothing prepared me for the message I heard just six days later in which God first called me ChristIAm! I had no recollection of the writing process at the beginning, but the messages were so loving and positive that I did not doubt that "Spirit God" was the speaker. I could not wait to hear more from *"God I Am, your co-creator, ever present with thee, within All That Is."*

For me the most difficult challenge has been speaking the name ChristIAm. I trusted what I heard no matter how hard it was to believe. But in our culture, in our churches, even in my family, I could expect and fear unwelcome results by claiming to be ChristIAm! The first few people with whom I shared the story and the name were more concerned than supportive. Later I allowed responsibilities and excuses to keep my journey private, at a safe distance, listening and writing but not sharing the messages or the name...

...for two decades! *"Slip and fall if you must, but do so knowing who you are."* I always trusted that hearing God's voice is *"just an intent away,"* and I sometimes listened. But it was only a few months ago that I had a wake-up call while reading page 262 of *Conversations with God: An Uncommon Dialogue, Book 3: Embracing the Love of the Universe*, by Neale Donald Walsch. It sent chills and goose bumps racing throughout my body.

In a conversation between God and Neale Donald Walsch, God declared that by not admitting that we are God, and by not acknowledging Who We Are, we deny God his rightful place within us *"three times before the cock crows"*— in our thoughts, words, and actions! I suddenly realized that I had been hiding behind fear all those years and would regret denying the voice of God within. It was time to accept the challenge and choose to share my spiritual journey!

Just three days later, Christine Kloser's unsolicited email arrived offering her Transformational Author Experience; it was obvious that it arrived right on time! My path is clear before me now. I have made a commitment to overcome fear of rejection, ridicule, and judgment; I will stop denying God! I will share the incredibly beautiful and significant messages I've received in dictation from the voice of God within, knowing that we all share, as One, the spiritual journey, the voice, and the Christ Self.

The significance of my story is not that I can hear the voice within and have been called ChristIAm. The significance is that YOU can hear God's voice within and we share the truth of Who We Are — ChristIAm! We are worthy! We are *"the Presence of God as Soul and Spirit manifesting in human form to experience the joy of Spirit truth."(Journal of ChristIAm, 8/22/89.)* Despite what we've been taught, we are not judged — ever! We are One with All That Is! We are Love and we are Life in Abundance!

Accepting these truths, what do we do next? What happens to me and you on ordinary days presently filled with jobs, kids, groceries, laundry, dirty dishes, and bills to pay, none of which seem possible to abandon? What do we do to be ChristIAm?

"...if one must abandon all that is the setting in which one moves about during the drama, then few will exit that scene to begin the journey; few will strike out on the path if they must immediately abandon all that is 'accumulated,' all that is 'accepted,' all that seems to be 'responsible.' And yet those conditions are simply qualities of the outer realm, whereas the journey is within. So you see ChristIAm, the question is its own answer... the challenge, and the joy of the journey to be made. For as one achieves a

knowingness in the inner real self, adjustments will be sought and achieved on the outer, but it is not necessary to give up 'all,' to 'abandon' all. Remember ChristIAm, the message is pure – the knowingness is who you are, and the Oneness of all with Spirit God. Your circumstances in the outer did not change – did not 'succeed' or 'fail,' while you allowed yourself to come into knowingness Beloved... but you will function with new understanding in the outer realm." – Spoken by Spirit God, March 24, 1989.

What can we do to become more trusting and powerful, more able to achieve all that we choose to be? What tools can help guide our moments?

"You have the power to feel as you desire at every moment. Affirm that to yourself whenever you have the slightest deviation from feelings of joy, and love, and positive thinking...

I have power to control how I feel at every moment, regardless of whatever experience seems to be in the moment. I choose to feel only love, joy, and peace toward myself and others.

I have power to create each moment in the image of the God I Am, from the level of consciousness that is Soul and Spirit, manifesting on the physical plane for the joy of experiencing Spirit truth.

I have power, I am joy, I am love, I am at One with the divine which is in All and is All; therefore no thing can come to me save the love and joy which I send forth.

I know who am I, and I accept the power that is mine to know my Christhood, and experience the treasures of divine peace, love and joy.

My name is ChristIAm. I am filled with the light of Spirit which I send forth as love to all.

I, (_____), am totally in control of the human vessel through the recognition that I am Soul, and I and Spirit are One, and I, Soul, and Spirit God, Creator of All, create each moment in fulfillment of my true desires. I have power over those desires, and the fulfillment of all that is desired. I accept that power, I am worthy of it, and only goodness can come from the awareness of who am I.

This day, my true Spirit self, takes power over conscious mind and the vessel, and acts each moment in peace, and love, and joy, recognizing the divinity in All.

I am peace; I am love; I am joy; I am One with All.

ChristIAm, these are powerful truths that have been spoken. Allow them to mold the moments of your day. Allow them to control your awareness and your emotions. I walk the path with thee at every moment, and long to see you in joy."– Spoken by Spirit God, February 13, 1989.

You might ask how anyone can "slip and fall" for two decades after hearing these messages. Why isn't it easy to trust and act on the truth of Who We Are? I ask myself that question constantly in my struggle to release fear and self-judgment. It seems as though it should be easy now that I know Who I Am. I've decided it must be like riding a bicycle – it doesn't look hard, but at first there are many failed attempts until there's a moment when it works, and soon after it is second nature. I've been assured by God that success is inevitable. We will all come to know Who We Are and achieve the Christ Self. I've been told there is no time; there is no hurry! The journey is the goal and all adds to the emotional experience that is heaven on earth.

"For you, conscious mind, are the gateway of I Am upon the physical plane. And when conscious mind allows the adventures of the physical plane to be experienced in purity of emotion, I Am is enriched beyond knowingness.... The point of it is that every scene, every one of them, enables Soul to experience truth, and by the emotion of it, to add to wisdom." – Spoken by Spirit God, September, 18, 1989.

Our story, my spiritual journey and yours, goes forward this day and the next. It is a pleasure sharing it with you! WE are Christ I Am in Oneness with Spirit God and All That Is! It is awesome, isn't it?! I will no longer deny God this rightful place. I will share what I hear God speak within because doing so mirrors the truth that you can listen, too. It is our truth together as One. This chapter ends with one of my favorite messages. I call it "Sunlight and Rain." It is especially pertinent to the challenges, struggles, and heartbreaks that prepare us for our greatest transformations toward Christ Consciousness.

Sunlight and Rain

"Beloved one, I speak to you. Arise from the peace which you be wearing like a slumber, and share in our communion. Beloved, your out-of-doors be dreary and dark this morning, and even the inner you senses the absence of sunlight, though you know the truth of the joy which be the miracle of rain I bring forth to nourish the earth, and the things of the earth. And you sense the balance of sunlight and rain, and the need for both. For in truth, the absence of either sunlight or rain would be devastating to life all about you.

Beloved, examine this truth and place it against the fabric of self in the physical. In truth, you hunger for the sunlight, to the exclusion of rain and 'dreary' days as you name them. Beloved, I sense that you absorb drops of truth as hungrily as the earth absorbs the rain. And you know the value to self of the 'rain' in your life, and of the beauty to Soul which be the 'dreary' moments. Beloved, if you can withhold judgment of your moments, and simply allow them; when you can be in any moment, in total recognition of the value of sunlight and rain, then you shall soak up the opportunities in the outer that be food for your growth into true knowingness of Spirit self.

This be a short lesson, Beloved. And I shall keep our communion pure — focused on the truth of the lesson of sunlight and rain. For you have much need to look out into the rain and the sky, which be not dreary but be filled with the gift of life. When you thus experience this truth, you shall attain great power over the outer — the power which takes the sunlight and the rain, and makes of them rainbows which be the pot of gold — the treasures of divine truth. Today in your moments, Beloved, notice that in every drop of rain is contained that same rainbow, and you shall be enriched beyond knowingness. You shall experience the outer moments in knowingness of the beauty in every moment, whether it be hidden within a drop of rain or be blazoned across the horizons. Go into the day dressed in this peace, Beloved!" — Spoken by Spirit God, April 11, 1990.

Marilyn Garrett, former librarian, teacher, and realtor, published *Journal of ChristIAm* in 1991. She leads guided imagery and meditation, and enjoys sharing focus, relaxation, and imagery with children. Marilyn knows you can hear God's voice, too; most already do, though they may doubt themselves or fear admitting it. Her website, www.GodSpeaksWithin.com, offers techniques and a forum for sharing this experience plus ChristIAm messages. You may request a complimentary full-color frameable version of "Sunlight and Rain."

From Victim to Empowered Agent for Transformation and Love

Bridgit Charandura Gooden

GRACE IS A POWERFUL FORCE THAT HAS infused my life even when I was utterly oblivious to its presence. Who would have thought the church's own "mulatto-bastard" child born during the revolutionary struggle in Rhodesia would end up owning her own business in the USA?

I chose to enter this earth on the most challenging of terms. I was born of a secret love of the unlikeliest pair in the Roman Catholic Church: two people who had been sworn to celibacy and dedicated their lives to serving God. My mother was a twenty-two-year-old native Catholic nun, and my dad was a Marist brother – a missionary educator more than twice her age from Canada. When the church personnel learned of my mother's pregnancy, they made her an offer she could not accept – that of giving me up for adoption by the church. When they could not work something out, she was asked to leave the convent with no real preparation for the outside world.

After learning of her pregnancy, my mother's parents disowned her. She had no one to turn to. My fetus cells absorbed all of the fear, shame, and guilt that my mother carried throughout her pregnancy. Soon after I was born, my father was shipped back to Canada where he continued to work as a Marist brother. Throughout my childhood I felt abandoned by my father. I felt it was my fault that my parents could not be together, and that I did not deserve to be loved. I also felt that I didn't have the right to be on earth. In almost every situation, except in the company of my mother, I felt like an outsider looking in.

Though my grandparents came to their senses after I was born, my life continued to be challenging throughout the years to come. I experienced the untimely deaths of my biological parents, a grandfather, a stepfather, and my first love, all by the age of twenty-eight. I was also inappropriately touched by my mother's boyfriend, and became the "holder" of this and other family secrets at a very young age. I continued the tradition of being the bearer of secrets into my adult life, even creating some of my own. I took all the pain from loss, my childhood shame and fears, plus abandonment issues, and stuffed them deep into my subconscious mind. Even though I never became a professional actor, I learned at a very young age how to pretend to be someone I was not in order to survive.

My primary focus from an early age was to become indestructible and do everything I could to prove that I deserved to be loved. I developed a sweet personality and put everyone else before me. I became the ultimate people pleaser and a relentless perfectionist. I unknowingly became a martyr, until one day when a mentor asked me, "What do you want out of life?" I looked at him with what felt like big saucer eyes, wondering, "What does he mean? Has he lost his mind? What planet did he come from? Oh wait... what do I want? I have no idea! I should know this!" I felt a wave of bewilderment interwoven with sadness. Throughout my entire life no one had ever asked me this vital question. It had never occurred to me that I had the right to determine and express what I wanted out of life. I had been giving my power away.

Fortunately, at that point in my life, I had been introduced to the practice of yoga. Svadhyaya, a yogic practice of self-study, became a very powerful tool for discovering who was hiding behind the mask that had almost permanently sealed itself onto my face. Yoga, and later meditation (part of the eight-limbed path of yoga), taught me many things: how to sit with myself and breathe; how to use breath to soften things in my physical body; how to use breath to access my emotional body, which was buried so deep it was almost nonexistent; how to be gentle, forgiving, compassionate, and loving toward myself; and how to surrender and systematically shed the armor that I had donned for many years while refraining from self-judgment or criticism.

Sometimes I'd remove a piece of the armor and almost immediately feel too vulnerable, and I'd grab it and stick it back on. I learned early from my yoga teachers that this was okay. It simply meant I wasn't ready, and there was no need to be self-critical or self-deprecating as a result.

I'd been taking classes for a while before I decided to try my own self-practice of yoga. On that morning I found a quiet place, moved through some warm-ups, and eventually into a pretty strong back-bending practice known for its energetic quality of "heart-opening." Afterward I felt open in my body and was very pleased with myself. However, I might have opened things up too quickly because later that afternoon a flood of emotions consumed me. I walked into a co-worker's office and burst into tears. Almost immediately, that critical voice inside me showed up saying, "This isn't the place for a senior data analyst working in a corporate office to have an emotional breakdown." Fortunately the co-worker was a close friend who lovingly tried to calm me down.

This experience scared me. I was afraid of my emotions and of becoming a "basket case." Being a problem solver, I was not used to dealing with issues for which I could not find a solution. I was afraid of tears. I had only seen my mother cry twice in her life: once at her father's funeral, and then when she was bidding me goodbye as I returned to the USA. I thought the second instance strange, but later learned that was the last time I would see her alive. She must have instinctively sensed something that I did not. So when I found myself crying at work, I believed tears to be a sign of weakness that I could not bear. In an attempt to hold on to some semblance of control, I abandoned my self-practice and decided to stick with taking classes, as they did not affect me as deeply. I was happy with my baby steps, but deep down I knew I had a lot of unprocessed emotions that would need to be addressed at some point.

It wasn't until later that I shared with my meditation teacher, Elesa Commerse, that I had not really allowed myself the time to properly mourn my mother's death. She responded by saying, "You should never hold back your tears. Tears are the voice of your soul." This statement touched the very core of my being, and I realized that I was actually stifling my soul's expression by forcing myself to be stoic and resisting "weakness." I thought I was being strong, when in fact I was being violent against myself and causing myself internal harm. The vulnerability I was running from was actually the path to courage I'd been seeking. As I shifted my perspective, it became clear to me that the times I'd perceived as embarrassing displays of weakness were actually those of bravery and authenticity!

After accepting my sensitivity as an asset, I realized that in almost all my moments of courageous self-expression my words were intermittent with bouts of tears, or the words flowed soon after a particularly tearful experience.

When I allow myself to connect with that place deep inside of me and don't shy away from my tears, I surprise myself by what flows almost effortlessly from my heart. I seem to become a clear channel for God's infinite wisdom. I simply have to stay present and let myself be vulnerable to the great unknown. Who knew?!

Elesa Commerse, for me, is the teacher who showed up when "the student was ready." She has nurtured me, presented me with challenging questions, helped foster my self-study, and nudged me to seek my internal truth. Through self-study I have been discovering my true nature. I am learning what it means to surrender, discern, be vulnerable, forgive, trust, have faith, be compassionate, listen with the heart, and experience the meaning of love. I am still a work in progress when it comes to spiritual growth, and I know my entire life on earth will be that of learning, growing, sharing, expanding, and evolving. My deep desire for transformation and connection continues to grow with each step I take. This to me is being human. This is what I came to earth to do! I am dedicated to my spiritual journey and to helping others discover theirs.

Through this process of letting myself be vulnerable, letting go of the need to be perfect, letting go of the need to be indestructible, and letting go of self-judgment, I came to observe the ever-present flow of grace in my life — even in the darkest of times. I started to notice all of the moments I was magically carried out of danger's path. I learned that the shameful experiences of my childhood later served as a catalyst that propelled me to seek my spiritual path. These experiences were "gifts wrapped in sandpaper," as one of my favorite authors, Lisa Nichols, calls them. They made me a more sensitive human being. They made me feel more deeply — not only my own pain, but that of others. They made me a more compassionate and loving being. They made me who I am today.

Dealing with my pain and fears has allowed me to inch a bit closer to God – to step into Divine Love and have the courage to embark on a journey of self-actualization on this beautiful planet. I now know that these experiences will allow me to connect more deeply with others and become a more powerful healer and agent for transformation and love. All I needed to do was shift my perspective, trust in my abilities, step out of my own way, and let God's grace lead me.

If you can relate to my story and would like to step out of your own way, take the following five simple action steps:

- **Get To Know Your True Self**

  I do self-study via yoga, meditation, reading personal-growth and spiritual-growth books and scripture, journaling, and, more recently, the Soul Voice® work created by Karina Schelde. If you don't know where to start, ask yourself on a daily basis three questions posed by one of my beloved yoga teachers, Aadil Palkhivala: 1) Who am I? 2) Why am I here? 3) Where am I going? No need to answer the questions. Simply ask them with sincerity, and then pay attention!

- **Get To Know God/Source/Your Higher Power**

  Discover your unique relationship with your Higher Power. What you call this force is irrelevant. (If you get hung up on what to call this force, you are hung up on judgment, which contracts your energy and prevents growth.) Allow yourself to explore how you best communicate with your Higher Power. Is it through prayer, meditation, sitting in silent contemplation, singing devotional songs, chanting, drumming, being in nature, journaling, creating art? You will be able to gain wisdom and feel a wave of calm, confident knowing when you've found your medium of communication.

- **Get To Know Your Unique Purpose**

  If you don't already know what it is, ask and your purpose shall be revealed to you. I asked my close group of girlfriends to help me figure out what my purpose was. After devoting one of our "Girls' Night In" monthly gatherings to discovering purpose, things in my life started to magically shift. If you ask out loud (or in writing) with sincerity, and remain open to what comes up, you will be surprised at how the whole Universe seems to come to your aid. Beware! The answers my not be what you expect.

- **Work on Opening Your Heart to Unconditional Love**

  What does the term *unconditional love* mean to you? Contemplate, pray, journal, and sit with this term. Be prepared to do some serious work on yourself. It starts with you. It's impossible to love others unconditionally when you don't love yourself. Believe me I have tried! The work includes forgiveness of self and others; asking forgiveness of those you've wronged (even if it's just energetically); developing compassion and gratitude; discovering your wounded inner child, your happy inner child, and your sense of playfulness and adventure; and locating and releasing the pain and negative emotions that are lodged in your body (via whatever medium available to you). It also includes discerning your unique and authentic self-expression, allowing your soul to shine and your spirit to soar, and encouraging others around you to do the same.

- **Work on Sharing Your Gifts with the World**

  Once you begin working on the steps above and remain with pure intentions, you will grow to realize that part of your purpose includes sharing your gifts and talents with others. As you continue on your spiritual-growth journey, more people and events that are aligned with your intentions will show up in your life. Join groups of like-minded people and share your unique self with them. You will be surprised by how many people's lives you will touch by simply being yourself. Your willingness to step into your power, and your desire to help the world become a better place, will invite God's grace to be more prevalent in your life. You will transcend your fears and anxieties and become the bold and brilliant being you were born to be. You will become an empowered agent of transformation and love.

In closing, I'll share thoughts from my most recent poem entitled "Desire to Love." Please enjoy and feel free to share it with your friends and family.

Desire to Love

My desire is to Love,
My desire is to Belong,
My desire is to deeply connect with all that is.

Let me step into the rays of Divine Light.
Let me whisper the Song of Life.
Let me share my tragedies, my victories, and my inner musings.
Let me listen to the sun's rays as they touch my face.
Let me dance on a raindrop.
Let me swim in the ocean of dreams.
Let me fly in the jungle of the great unknown.
Let me inspire a king to give up his worldly possessions.
Let me engage a beggar's wisdom.

Let us sing each other's stories.
Let us paint a rainbow on a tree.
Let us create a new reality of harmony and compassion.
Let us dine, sing, and dance with the dolphins.
Let us wade waters with the lions.
Let us share our deepest desires with the weeds.
Let us be plucked by the roses.
Let us drop pretenses and speak from the heart.
Let us forgive, move on, and love abundantly.

My desire is to deeply connect with all that is,
My desire is to Belong,
My desire is to Love.

Bridgit Charandura Gooden, a Zimbabwean-born economics major turned Pilates/yoga/meditation teacher, lives in Chicago. Born into a family ridden with loss and secrets, she silenced her voice and chose a career that kept her safe from being seen or heard. However, the Universe had other plans, and once she surrendered to God's call, Bridgit was inspired to become an agent for transformation and love around the world. For a free thirty-minute consultation, please contact Bridgit via www.CTransformations.com.

All Is Well with My Soul

Christina Haas

IT WAS A GORGEOUS FALL MORNING, just after Thanksgiving, as I walked through my neighborhood. The last five-and-a-half years had marked a period of intense change and transformation for me. Finally balance was returning to my life and things were not so hard. I felt myself smiling.

Moments later I noticed a large, brown mass up ahead on the side of the road. My demeanor shifted as I got closer. I saw a young deer, fatally wounded but still breathing ever so slightly. She had a last lesson to teach me before she died – a lesson about letting go and finally saying goodbye to the remnants of my old self.

Before her lesson will make sense, I need to go backwards in time. I was born in 1963, the oldest of three girls, to a Catholic father and a Lutheran mother. My family, the Catholic traditions, and the world around me formed a large part of who I was. The notion that children should be seen and not heard and the Catholic teaching that we are born sinners in need of redemption both had a large impact on my psyche. In the national community, the feminist movement gained significant momentum during my childhood years and my generation may very well have been the first in which girls truly believed they could be anything when they grew up.

By the time I graduated from college, I was on a business track, eventually earning my Certified Public Accountant (CPA) license and a master's in taxation. This outward manifestation of me was a stark contrast to who I was inwardly. I grew up with rules and logic, not spirit and intuition. The internal opposition grew bigger and bigger over the years until a miscarriage and a wake-up call in my marriage jarred me from my slumber.

My miscarriage in 2003 was the first significant event to trigger my internal realignment process. At that juncture in my life I had two happy and healthy children, a fourteen-year marriage, a job as president and part owner of a real estate management company, and I lived in a beautiful home in a seaside community south of Boston, Massachusetts. A surprise pregnancy in the fall of 2003 reminded me that I was not *really* in charge, driving that message home a mere three weeks later when I miscarried the baby. That loss, hard enough on its own, triggered memories of an abortion my husband and I had chosen earlier in our marriage, figuratively and literally bringing me to my knees. This was my first glimpse of knowing that I was unaligned with my soul, although at the time I don't think I realized how deep the rupture was. My husband did not understand and could not relate to my pain. My shame and pain were isolating and left me feeling alone and abandoned, thus I began the journey of healing from my abortion and miscarriage by myself. As I did that, the other illusions in my life slowly revealed themselves.

My marriage was the next illusion to be shattered. The relationship had always been incredibly hard work for me. From the beginning my husband had lied to me about his past. Although I knew in my heart that he was not telling the truth, the rescuer in me wanted to help him. I denied my intuition. A house built on lies is very hard to live in.

The abortion etched its secret into my heart and soul. As a Catholic woman, the unworthiness I felt eroded my personal boundaries so badly that I lost my individuality completely. My husband expected that I work, although I longed to devote myself to being a full-time mother. So I stayed home with my kids and worked from home, sometimes into the wee hours of the night, so that we could maintain our lifestyle. Managing the house, taking care of the chores — all of those details that are necessary for life to flow were my responsibility in addition to my job as president and chief financial officer of my real estate company.

I did everything without complaint, diminishing my health and well-being with each day, primarily because of the unworthiness and shame I carried from my abortion. My husband worked too, but still recreated; he took flying lessons, went boating, and eventually went back to school for church leadership. There was no mutuality in our relationship. By the time of our miscarriage, I had become a full-fledged doormat. A pivotal event in our marriage occurred paradoxically the night our daughter made her first holy communion, and proved just how little value I held for him. I knew from my post-abortion healing that we were not emotionally or spiritually connected. His inability to hear my voice or my body that night, both crying in pain, was proof that I was not physically present for him either. That night was the second indication that there was a chasm in my soul, a little bit deeper now for it had existed longer. It never occurred to me that I would someday be divorced. Neither my upbringing nor my religion sanctioned it. After two years of off-and-on marriage counseling, he finally moved out.

I thought that knowing our marriage was not salvageable would make the divorce process easy. I was terribly wrong. It was the longest piece of leaving behind parts of my life that were not serving me. It opened my eyes to realities in politics, the judicial system, and the patriarchal hierarchy of my faith tradition in ways I never could have imagined. It was during this time that I discovered that the Catholicism I had devoted much of my life to was incongruent with the essence of Jesus's teachings and my core beliefs. It was time to release my religion as I worked on dissolving the marriage. In the end it became obvious that I could no longer afford to keep the marital home, and so it was sold. After I had lost my home, office space, and subsequently my job, I finally received permission to leave the state and move to California to be near family. I went to California exhausted, but certain now that I would finally be able to finish realigning my body and soul.

I knew that as a single mother with my children's co-parent 3,000 miles away, I would now be parenting 24/7. I will be honest – while I knew that we all needed a fresh start, I was scared and did not believe I could parent entirely on my own. With my family nearby, I had a safety net. But I very quickly learned that while I harbored fantasies of being close, they had their own lives that did not readily welcome change. And I finally learned how it was that I had been so comfortable with my ex-husband for so long. I hadn't realized that the emotional inaccessibility and control in my marriage were similar to that which I had grown up with. I needed professional assistance to understand that I could not stay close to my family and still complete the process of coming back to myself. The last and most painful lesson I learned was that in order to discover my true self I would need to separate from my family. It was an unexpected and profound lesson that tested my strength once again.

All of these shattered illusions have put me face to face with issues of anger and forgiveness. Several books were serendipitously referred to me by friends, starting with Christel Nani's *Diary of a Medical Intuitive*. Later on, Brian Weiss's *Many Lives, Many Masters* and James Van Praagh's *Growing Up in Heaven* provided new and resonating perspectives. From watching Oprah's *Super Soul Sunday* I came across spiritual teacher Caroline Myss, and read and listened to hours of her teachings. With the grace of God and the mystical knowledge these spiritual teachers had to share, I have come to believe that everything I experienced was necessary and critical for my soul's journey. I could not know my own strength, listen to my intuition, or follow my guidance without these situations in my life. While I could stay angry, live in victim energy, and be an unforgiving person, I could also just as easily choose to look at these experiences as steps on the ladder of personal and spiritual growth. Everything that happened in my life that I had labeled "bad" was really a gift! Every relationship had a purpose, one which has strengthened me and brought me back to my spirit. What an extraordinary lesson! My kids here on earth and my children in heaven have been part of this lesson for me, too. I know that they chose me, they love me, and they each help me grow better every day.

I feel a passion now to work with women who have had abortions and help them release the secret they hold that keeps them from being full and joyful manifestations of themselves. Holding on to secrets makes us unhealthy, physically and emotionally. Christel Nani introduced her observations in *Diary of a Medical Intuitive* that women who have breast cancer all have at least one common link – holding on to a secret. I believe these secrets of the heart are one element of breast cancer that I hope we can cure in my lifetime. I also believe that the far right's attack on abortion clinics, doctors, and the pro-choice movement makes it hard for anyone with an abortion secret to open up about it.

We do not live in a perfect world. I have seen so many women in my job and in the courtroom who take care of children with little or no support from a partner. My country, the United States of America, has the second-highest child poverty rate of any developed nation in the world. I believe women know intuitively that abortion is sometimes a choice not between life and death, but between two tragic options. The captain of the Titanic was not vilified for having to choose who got on the lifeboats and who didn't. Soldiers returning from war are not maligned for death they meted out in their call of duty. Pregnant and post-abortive women need love, understanding, and support, not condemnation. Our lives are forever altered by pregnancy in a way that only we can understand.

As I walked through my neighborhood that late November Sunday morning, the tears that fell from my eyes told me clearly that there was still something undone to bring my soul completely into alignment. I sat with the deer that day as she finally passed from this world, her youth, gentleness, and grace leaving her physical body. As her belly stopped rising and she surrendered her spirit to God, my grief continued. It stayed with me for the rest of the day, continuing into the next. Finally, two days later, as I rode my bike past where I'd found the deer, I now knew what I needed to do. It was time for me to let go and submit to God, just as the deer had finally done two days earlier. I had already relinquished so much, but I still had not completely surrendered to God. I cried again as I acknowledged my fear and released my remaining worries and doubts to the ether. As I rode on, a new certainty came over me. There was nothing left to release now. I had surrendered everything. The hard part was over and the best was yet to come. I was smiling again, this time out loud and in my heart.

Finally, all is well with my soul.

Christina Haas, a former business owner and CPA, is an emerging voice for women of all ages who yearn to release the guilt, pain, and isolation of having an abortion. Through her own journey, Christina helps women experience forgiveness, healing, acceptance, and freedom around this sensitive issue. A natural cheerleader, she'll help you feel more connected to yourself and others as you learn how to live more fully as who you're meant to be. Learn more at www. AllIsWellWithMySoul.com.

Triumph Alchemy – Transforming Life's Challenges into Golden Accomplishments

Vivian Hanai

THE PURPOSE OF A WHOLE LIFETIME IS defined by a precious collection of deeply affecting events. They may last just a few minutes, perhaps only seconds, but they contain the purest essence of human existence, with its impressive ability to transcend space and time boundaries.

No matter how busy and chaotic the flow of events is — on the streets, at home, on social networks — some moments are so special they withstand the test of time and, by the simple command of memory, may be relived as clearly as being in a high-definition movie: the feeling of unconditional love in your mother's embrace; your father's strong and affectionate tone of voice when he taught you how to use a pen; the strangeness and the loneliness of your first school days; the warm touch of the sun and the noisy fun of a summer day on the farm in the company of your dearest cousins and friends; the nervousness and the pride felt along with the discovery of your first menstrual period; your heart's strong beat as you stood close to that one person who completely altered your perception of reality; the excruciating pain of being disappointed in love; the intoxicating glory of professional achievements; or the well-being and feeling of wholeness as your body responded to a sea breeze or the rain's refreshing perfume.

From the sacred space of "now," I would like to share with you a few of the most important movements I co-created with the Eternal One to transform my life into a masterpiece. They were crucial decisions that shaped my existence and influenced each of the results I have achieved so far. I will do my best to describe exactly all that has happened, and I kindly ask you to follow me with the eyes not only of the mind but of the spirit – the higher vision originating in the essence that unites us all in one universal consciousness and in one body of Light.[1]

Halfway through the year of 2006, I believed I was the happiest any woman could wish to be. I had a handsome, intelligent, and loving boyfriend with whom I managed our successful telemarketing business. We had a reliable staff of cheerful and competent members, and really enjoyed ourselves at home, at work, around town, and on travels wide and far.

All seemed perfect, but just the same I felt there was something missing, and I couldn't quite put my finger on it. It felt as if the life I was living was not my own. I looked out of a window and nothing seemed true. I sensed that what I could see, hear, and experience was a virtual reality, as inthe movie *The Matrix*.

Aiming at broadening my knowledge and widening my horizons, I enrolled in a drama course. On the very first day, a woman called Rachel[2] engaged in conversation with me. She was nice and pleasant, had an elegant posture, and there was this air of mystery about her. We talked about the course, our lives and aspirations, but my interest

1   Light refers to divine light, the source of everything that exists in the Universe.
2   Names have been changed to protect the privacy of the individuals involved.

really picked up when she mentioned her experience with angels, meditation, and the ancient Jewish school of mystic thought called the kabbalah. Though knowing nothing about the subject, the voice of my intuition whispered down in my depths that the kabbalah was the doorway to all of the answers I had been searching for all my life. Realizing how truly interested I was, Rachel suggested a book by a rabbi named Aryeh Kaplan and gave me specific instructions for a meditation exercise. In that very same week, I spent a whole night practicing the system meticulously until daybreak. As I finished the ritual, besides the good feeling of mission accomplished, I had the clear sensation that nothing would ever be the same again.

Time went on and my relationship with my boyfriend Peter[2] was becoming visibly frayed. His excessive materialism, self-centeredness, and lack of spiritual values were becoming all too evident, but affection and sexual involvement were still very intense. One day though, I found a shocking series of erotic messages exchanged between Peter and my administrative assistant. A sadist (or was it an angel?) had installed a software program that captured all MSN messages sent in the office and, as if that were not enough, published them all on my Orkut page – the biggest social network at the time – for everyone to see. It was too horrible to be true: my boyfriend was cheating on me with my best employee and friend, and to make matters worse, I suffered public humiliation at work and on the social network. All I wanted to do was run out of the office, or better yet, disappear from the face of the Earth. What kept me from taking a more drastic measure was the immense pain a definitive departure from this physical life would have caused my parents, relatives, and closest friends.

I returned to my apartment to pick up my personal things and then drove off to my mother's home, never to return to my former place or the office again. It was one of the most mortifying experiences in my life, but thankfully my mother received me with open arms. I had left behind the mainstays of my life: boyfriend, business, and home. My car, which I still had, became pretty useless, since I didn't even want to leave the house. I spent most of those days in deep slumber, nearly as deep as death itself.

I was aimless. I had no idea what to do with my life and the external world was meaningless to me. The most convenient alternative I found was devotion to prayers and meditation, hoping to recover and build up strength from my inner core. This was, after all, the only part of me that remained to lean on, since I was completely drained, mentally, emotionally, and physically.

Meanwhile, my friend Rachel was involved in a car accident and her nerves were shattered as a result of suffering several cuts to her hands and face. Since I wanted to help her and divert attention from my supposed disgrace, I paid a visit to her mentor, Luiz C. Kozlowski, to ask for help. Our meeting was magical; it seemed as if we had known each other for centuries. He not only advised me about how to help Rachel with her issues, but provided me with one of the most spectacular perspectives on self-knowledge, the dimensions of human existence, and purpose and mission in life.

One day in May of 2008, following months dedicated to meditation and studies of alchemy, the kabbalah, and the Great White Brotherhood, I decided to fast for twenty-four hours in order to concentrate all my vital strength on contacting and experiencing other levels of consciousness and reality.

I was in my bedroom sitting in the lotus position. My body felt so light and subtle, as if it had sublimated and entered the gaseous state to the point that it became mixed with air particles. At the same time I had the sensation of not being there. In that deep state of meditation, my mind was serene to the point of stillness. There were no thoughts, only a deeply ingrained and overwhelming feeling of well-being and a state of complete union with the Almighty, the Eternal, and the Universe.

That is when I noticed the majestic presence of a crystalline being in the left corner of the bedroom. He was about six feet tall, had long hair, and wore garments reminiscent of both a kimono and medieval armor. I was unable to determine the texture of his clothing, skin, or hair because I saw him as a structure of vector lines, as if he were a marvelous, transparent, animated drawing superimposed on the bedroom scenery, radiating intense white light. He had a look of strong determination. Though he had no wings, I wish to call him an angel just the same. He brought orders from the highest echelon: the Most High himself.

I was fully enjoying that unique experience of making contact with a being from another dimension. I had watched movies about and heard reports from people who had somehow been in contact with spirits, angels, or ETs, and had wondered what my reaction would be should anything like that happen to me. I was divided between my rational side, claiming, "This is nothing but a Hollywood invention. These people are lying or hallucinating, and all they want is to be seen," and the voice of my intuition, stating, "Interesting... I've known all along that there is more to this world than our five senses can inform us of. How would I react if that happened to me? I would expect to be calm and peaceful so as to interact in a most productive and beneficial way."

- "Do you want to have a son?" asked the angel telepathically.

- "What do you mean by a son? I'm not ready for one. I don't even have a boyfriend," I answered hesitantly.

- "He's called David. Do you want to or not?"

- "If you've gone to the trouble of showing up in my bedroom just to say that to me, who am I to say I don't? Oh yes, I do want to!"

- "The father is Luiz."

As this last sentence was uttered, the Light presence vanished, and I was overcome with spiritual strength and the magnificent certainty that nothing and no one would be able to get me off course. On the following day, in one of the lounges of an international hotel where Luiz could often be found sitting at a table in a corner, I walked over to him and without a single greeting, went straight to the point:

- "You are the father of my son."

I thought he would react with great surprise at such an inordinate statement. He did not move a single facial muscle, though, and answered with great calm,

- "I know."

The next day, Luiz C. Kozlowski and I were living together. In a very private ceremony, with only the two of us, we pledged not only to devote ourselves to each other and our families, but to use our gifts to serve humanity, particularly by promoting excellence and the Triumph Alchemy at four levels: physical, emotional, mental, and spiritual. Three months later I was happily pregnant with David. He was born beautiful, healthy, and full of life on April 8, 2009, the special Jewish date of Birkat Hachamah (the Blessing of the Sun). Today I am aware that my life is full of meaning, that I am on the pathway aligned with my life's purpose, and that the reality of my surroundings has never been so wonderfully true, complete, and divinely magical.

I believe the noblest mission in life is to recognize, polish, keep, and lovingly share the most consequential moments of pain and pleasure, for the experiences with the greatest impact are as valuable as diamonds. We all carry within ourselves a treasure trove replete with these precious stones — all we have to do is acknowledge them. The shine and splendor of each gem increases as we work at expanding our consciousness and developing our ability to manifest the fruits of such evolution in our daily activities. In this way we change ourselves and, consequently, the life and the world around us.

As we consciously use the divine power of our desire and imagination, we can face each challenge as if it were a jewel. We can see it as an opportunity to reveal the golden Light that definitively exists in each point of our being, especially in the darkest spots. Whether you want them or not, you have inherited the tools and the essence of the greatest alchemist of all times — The Eternal, God Father-Mother, The Unknowable. It is time to remember your true origins, to vibrate in unison with them, and shine brightly like a diamond!

Heaven is being created right now on Earth and it abounds with Triumph Alchemists.

Vivian Hanai is Divine Inspiration and President of Merkabah Empire — Sustainable and Human Development Association. She is the co-creator of Triumph Alchemy™, a method that focuses on fully reintegrating human beings into the Original Source. The techniques improve physical, emotional, mental, and spiritual awareness in order to promote excellence in every aspect of life, including: self-esteem, love and relationships, and financial freedom. You are invited to express your full potential, inspire those around you, and co-create Heaven on Earth at MerkabahEmpire.org.

The Alchemy of Connection – Through Life, Death, and Rebirth

At the Heart of Challenge Lies Grace – Embrace Your Sound of
Silence and Rebirth the Language of Your Soul

Katrine Legg Hauger
Lawyer, Certified Constellator, Alchemy Storyteller

THIS IS A STORY OF DEEP LISTENING – of deep transformation and dignity. My inner knowledge always knew that there are no limits to what we can achieve together, that we are all connected, that we are all love, and that we are all held. I trusted this with my heart and bones, yet my throat was blocked when it came to my true knowing. I felt different. I felt alone. Was it only me?

I hid the true me. My voice chronically left me. The Universe worked hard but gracefully to help me own and integrate my story, dare my courage, and become my inner voice.

I am an alchemist run by forces of universal co-creation, connectedness, and synchronicities. I am one. I am home and free. I belong in the presence of many. I am a voice for you to feel beyond reasoning and thinking. We share the same cosmic nervous system. We share the same stars. From heart to heart, I hope you feel my words. From Soul to Soul we are one with the silence.

I'd like to share with you lines from the song "Sounds of Silence" by Paul Simon, one of my father's favorite artists:

"And in the naked light I saw
Ten thousand people, maybe more
People talking without speaking
People hearing without listening
People writing songs that voices never share
And no one dared
Disturb the sound of silence."

Our Souls know that right now is the greatest moment of listening, receiving, and choice we have ever faced together as a human species. I humbly and respectfully invite you to cultivate your heart's listening and your Soul's voice in this time of continual rebirthing of our planetary conscious evolution. We are the ones we have been waiting for to initiate positive change.

Your life challenges and struggles are preparing you for your higher mission. The old ways of living and doing business are over. The new economy, regulations, and systems are what really matter — your family, parenting, education, clean water, and healthy food.

Competition and ego-driven profit belong to the past. It's time to live, parent, love, lead, and build your life, business, and community with encouragement and responsibility in alignment with who you truly are. It's time for a sacred, feminine, collaborative, systemic approach, and sharing the generosity deep in our hearts. It's time to manifest your birthright, namely personal and financial freedom and abundance, so you can give back and be the difference in the world that you wish to see.

Many people have had huge wake-up calls over the past few years. They were, like me, urged to start healing their Souls and investing in what really matters — that which can only be found by looking into your heart. I believe if you're still reading this, then some resonance is touching some part of you — the part that wants to explore more — even if you don't exactly understand the what, why, or how. Yes, it gets challenging at times. But when those times happen, instead of surviving by avoiding or distracting yourself from whatever you're feeling, sit, close your eyes, take a few deep breaths, and surrender into it. Let yourself feel, receive, and express what's happening in the process to let it be.

I believe in a comprehensive, integrative approach to being who we are meant to be. This all-encompassing approach is how we heal, enhance, and rebirth the new thought, enlightenment, and financial freedom we all desire. Everything needs to realign with source, purpose, clarity, and focus.

The misalignment between the Soul and the body is where struggle lives. As you do the inner work of coming into alignment, the struggle dissipates. I know how painful that process can be, yet if you want to heal yourself and humanity, and co-create a sustainable world for all, coming into alignment is a necessary process. We are all, with our unique purposes, stories, and experiences, building blocks for this new planetary shift... one person at a time.

When I was out of alignment within myself, my life was very challenging. I experienced life-threatening meningitis that ended in my being in a coma at age sixteen; a medical breast reduction at nineteen; a laser operation to treat chronically losing my voice for a period of fifteen years; infertility problems and operations; and tough pregnancies ending in acute caesarean sections. All of these challenges were connected to not truly being who I really was and not using the knowledge and gifts I knew I had within, combined with deep unconscious acts due to loss and the entanglements of blind love to my family system.

My true awakening and inner spiritual journey into alignment started when I began to listen to my inner voice and our children, entering my stillness and my moon and integrating and acknowledging all there is as it is. I healed myself back to my source, found my true self-love, and started manifesting my Soul gifts and planetary visions of human remembering.

Following are some excerpts from my personal journals that I hope will help open you in exploring the alchemy in your own life.

The Autumn Moon of 2004: Birthing the New Seeds of Hope and Possibility — A New Moon

After I tried to get pregnant for a couple of years, the doctors said I needed an operation to remove endometriosis. I knew I never wanted another operation again. So I started visiting a natural therapist. For months I kept asking, "Can't you just put those needles in my uterus?" She said, "No. You are not ready." One day she said, "Now you are ready!" Our daughter was conceived on the full moon night the same day.

We were so grateful, but my body had a hard time managing the pregnancy. Towards the end I was pushed around in a wheelchair. The doctors decided an acute cesarean section was necessary. Our wonderful healthy daughter was born in June.

The Autumn Moon of 2006: Mothership of Many

We followed the advice of the doctors to inseminate one of our seven fertilized frozen egg cells, ending in an early miscarriage. However, to our surprise, we once more got pregnant naturally after that! Our beautiful son was healthy, but the pregnancy and birth were identical to my first. The operation wounds healed, but I can still remember feeling the morphine in my thighs. My weight increased from 121 pounds to 242 pounds, and I could hardly walk.

Autumn Moon of 2008: The First Voices of Channeling the Sudden Loss of My Father

Our children are sitting next to their grandfather in the airplane, pointing out into the skies. My father is wearing his sixpence hat as usual. He is telling them that they will meet his parents and see England where he grew up. I had followed my intuition to book these flights for December 2nd, despite the challenge it took to travel at that time.

The early morning of December 4th, my father passed away. The doctors never found the cause of death. Everything was normal the day before. Was this why I had suddenly put all our plans, Christmas preparations, my new job, and my husband's work aside to go to England?

Feeling the numbness in my toes, wisdom teeth, and hair, I was in shock, yet I felt my inner wisdom and an accepting calmness. My grandparents were to live longer than their son. He was only sixty years old. My father is home again, finally in peace. My grandparents got their son back in England after he'd spent nearly thirty-six years in Norway. The circle is closed. This was the start of trusting my source-guided journey into new realms and realities through believing my intuition.

My father. Looking like a child sleeping in the bed in his parents' bungalow. He is sleeping on his side with his head on the pillow. His right arm is under the pillow and sticking straight out past the edge of the bed. His face is peaceful. He is still in the room. His loving hand is turned slightly towards the ceiling, ready to be held. By me.

The silence is stoic. Humility, deep gratefulness for life, and the purest love fills me and the room. Words are not needed. I mention our children. I am thanking my father for everything. We will manage. Tranquility and peace. Sending love and acceptance through his hand. I am.

I have flashbacks to the theater performance I invited our father to come with us to see two months earlier. A childhood friend is giving a one-person performance entitled *My Name Is Rachel Corrie*. At one moment she shared a piece of paper that was passed around in the audience. I started crying when I saw the simple pencil sketch of the civil peace activist who died on the border of Gaza, lying on the ground with his right arm pointing straight up in the air. It made a huge impression on me. It was days before I could let go of the strong impression. The arm. I keep holding my father's outstretched arm.

After our last farewell before cremation, we noticed the sky was low with a distinct linear arrow formation. The edges were clear, and formed a big triangular low-light ceiling above the bungalow. This was the work of a true architect similar to what my father was in life. We have never seen anything like it before or after. He was telling us that he is in peace and that he loves us, a last greeting to everyone.

The Spring Moon of 2011: The Silent Voices of the Unborn

One night I could not sleep; I knew I needed to ask for a Family Constellation, not knowing why or what would happen. (A Family Constellation is a phenomenological, multi-generational method, unveiling hidden solutions and movements of the Souls in the morphic field, enabling clients to see and integrate the reality as it is with love and to release and resolve profound tensions, entanglements, and imbalances within and between people.)

My intention was to restore balance in my family, and the intention, my husband, myself, and our born children were set up with representatives as is done with Family Constellations. Not much happened in the beginning with the representatives. The one who was the intention fell to the floor. We were all tired and frustrated.

Then came what I today call our unborn children, our six deep-frozen, fertilized egg cells. One by one they appeared by representatives... the Souls of these unborn children were instantly warmly embraced by our son, who could not let them go. They were all cold and shivering, and asked for a warm carpet. The Soul of our miscarried child also showed up and wanted to be included. Two of them were desperately willing to live; two were begging to be destroyed, as they did not want to wait and freeze anymore; the others disappeared into the corners of the big room. Our born children had very strong connections with a couple of their unborn siblings.

With tears in our eyes we told our unborn children that they were deeply loved and wanted, but that my body had been too weak. Their eyes were touched, filled with love, wonder, delight, and relief. All our nine children needed to be together, seen, heard, and acknowledged to finally get peace and their correct place in our family system. It was a true healing gift to feel and observe the connectedness among all the children, and be able to look them in the eyes. These Souls were part of my own and my family's truth. These Souls belong. If we didn't listen and include them, our family would be in imbalance and the pain, sorrow, and symptoms in my body would persist. It was divine and graceful.

I remembered the strong intuition I'd had the last years — an inner calling and wish for having more children that my mind could not understand. I felt this taboo longing for the unborn children even though we had our wonderful son and daughter. My body would not let go of being in a state of giving birth, nor could I shed the extra weight.

The evening after the constellation, my husband amazingly opened up to checking out the procedure for insemination. I called the hospital to get a status on what would happen and the destruction date. A bioengineer checked the register and said that the destruction deadline was yesterday! The day after the constellation! She said the European Union regulations are very strict, and that they destroy all eggs on the very day, five years after they are frozen. I was shocked and asked her to check on whether they had been destroyed. She checked and replied that they actually had not been destroyed even though they should have been. I prayed for them not to be destroyed and that they would let us insert the eggs. I called the hospital the next day and they would not let us insert the eggs even though they had not been destroyed. The date was absolute and they could have lost their license if they made an exception. The timing of it all was pure alchemy. I lost my extra weight only a few weeks after this constellation, and my family was finally at peace.

* * *

This awakened me to the challenges of today's new fertilization technology; the Souls of the unborn, parents, and siblings carrying the unknown burdens and consequences of unborn life. As a lawyer I had created and worked with regulatory frameworks for years. Are we manipulating the miracles of life? Are we underestimating the dignity and memories of Souls? Was there a lack of a humanistic approach in our regulatory framework?

Was my strong intuition of the last years right? Had my body healed as quickly as it had to be able to welcome the unborn children? Were these destinies part of my entanglements in blind love and loyalty for my ancestors who could not live and had never been recognized? Was this a lesson of respect for life and death? A lesson for our society and humanity? A lesson for a lawyer like me?

I bow for you, our beloved child. I bow for the womb of mother earth. I bow for the universal trust of the unknown outcome of birthing and rebirthing each and every Soul. We all belong.

My advice is to practice listening and journaling. In this way you alchemize your presence and purpose for true deep healing, health, sustainability, abundance, and peace.

Here are a few ways to cultivate the language of your body and Soul:

- Be in stillness and ask for your emptiness.
- Breathe deeply, focusing on your breath.
- Enter the sacred space deep within your heart.
- Receive your presents in your presence.
- Listen deeply to what emerges – a word, picture, or awareness beyond thought or expression.
- Express gratitude for any deep inner knowing.
- Embrace negative emotions and acknowledge the grace of receiving what is being born.
- Identify your deepest vibrational resonance in your life.
- Trust your inner knowledge.
- Never fear your own remembrance, as you are never alone. You are held.

- "You take two bodies and you twirl them into one, their hearts and their bones, and they won't come undone." — Paul Simon, "Hearts and Bones"

Katrine Legg Hauger is an alchemist whose mission is the co-creation of a New Wave Paradigm on our planet. Her thought leadership on spirituality, health, and wealth guide conscious leaders, individuals, and professionals to find self-worth, connectedness, autonomy, clarity, courage, and direction to thrive in the new economy and create vibrant health and wealth with divine purpose. Katrine teaches globally to bring about new awareness and solutions for spiritual and systemic healing. For speaking engagements, events, books, and sessions, visit www.QuantumBodySoulAlchemy.com.

The Secrets and Shadows of Lost Understanding

Angela Hiroshima, CECF

When Our Soul Asks Us to Speak

I PACE UPSTAIRS IN MY BEDROOM, wearing a path in the carpet under my nervous feet. As I walk in yet another loop with my throat closing in, I can only focus on the breathlessness in my lungs and the heaviness of my head on my shoulders. I should feel relief knowing this is the day I've anticipated for over a decade, but instead I am overcome with the sensation of vertigo, like I am teetering on the edge of a cliff. How will she respond? What will she do? I can't take this pressure. This isn't how it was supposed to go. God, please don't let me screw this up. She wasn't supposed to find the certificate in the photo album at her great grandma's house. Mom and Dad, Grandma, Aunty... they say I should tell her; that mistakes happen.

I need courage. *Breathe* I think, as nausea sets in.

How will I tell her that the life she knows is a lie? That there is a lifetime of secrets being held from her by the people she trusted the most?

In this moment, our worlds will change forever. I start to pray.

A Silent Foundation

I come from a multicultural home, with a Japanese father and a Swedish mother. My youth was a paradox between the outspoken, freethinking, and individualistic American culture, and the conservative, soft-spoken, respectful, and demure Japanese one.

As a young girl, my voice was not as loud and expressive as a typical American girl's. It was closer to a low hum. Japanese girls are taught to be demure, and in my home certain topics were not discussed.

I was also raised with Christian values, with a faith in a God I could not understand but knew I was supposed to respect. My relationship with spirit felt like a lesson plan for "how to be good," and I took it seriously. Hell was a real place in my mind, and I wasn't going to land there if I could help it. I also had a strong desire to please my parents. Good girls are expected to not create a stir.

I would create a stir.

Age Seventeen

In my junior year of high school, thirty seconds changed my life.

I knew what sex was in theory, and I knew that there were risks. But he looked *great* in football gear. That's all that crossed my mind before I jumped head-first into a moment that altered the course of the rest of my life.

Later that year, after a quick and anxious statement from our family doctor, my mother sat down, put her head between her legs, and proceeded to hyperventilate. She thought I was there to get a simple physical, so you can imagine my family's surprise when it was announced that I was pregnant and almost full term.

Thud.

My family needed to catch their breath, but there was no time. Shock set in, followed by quick decisions and an absent mourning period. When my mother came up for air a few days later, she offered me a solution: my parents could adopt my baby. What? Adopt my baby and keep her in the family? I felt relief, and sick to my stomach.

"Wait!" It was all happening too fast. But babies don't wait. Decisions had to be made.

A cascade of worry became a barrage of questions in my mind. *How will this turn out? Do I want my daughter to be raised like I was? How will I handle this every day?*

For some families, this is a perfect solution. There are many stories of happy endings. What's the worst thing that can happen?

I agreed to this solution with as much understanding and awareness as my panicked seventeen-year-old mind could process. Keeping this baby in the family felt like a reasonable solution. She would be loved, I wouldn't lose the chance to know her, and I could continue my education. I never thought about the impact of an actual adoption, or why it was the only solution my mother offered. To me it meant help and relief. So my parents adopted my daughter, and I grew up.

Life Plans are Fickle Friends

My parents and I agreed to tell my daughter the truth about her life's origins before she started school. We hoped that at that age, she could adjust and develop relationships with her family members in their original capacities.

Then the **it hit the fan.

Just a few short years after the adoption, my parents decided to go their separate ways. Our family plan was derailed. The comfort of knowing that both my parents were involved in my daughter's life disintegrated.

My mother's twenty-five years of marriage had been severed. Her desire to do what was necessary in the face of a massive life change created a need for her to not only survive, but to start anew. Her solution was to move away, and she took my daughter with her.

This changed the course of my life once more.

My parents included me in the initial discussion, but my mother's final decision was made alone. My mom wanted to raise my daughter; her rights stated that she could; it was done.

I hadn't come to peace with my decision to let my daughter be adopted, and this news brought a new struggle – I had to let go of the physical connection, and I wasn't prepared for that. My heart was breaking with the realizations that flooded in. The choice I had made with the best intentions became a sentence. For the second time in my life, I clearly saw the consequences of my choices. There was no discussion, no communication, and now my world was split into a deep chasm. I fell straight to the bottom.

Sleeping in until the afternoon and staying up late at night became my pattern. I got lost in the nightlife of dancing, music, and superficial glitz. It seemed to quell the pain. I slept most of the day away until I could drown out my pain in the noise of nightlife. I wanted love, attention, distraction – something to ease the feelings of a void and the loneliness one feels when life appears to turn its back. I had walked my daughter's young soul into a nightmare, and feared she would never forgive me for agreeing to leave her to a life that was less than what she deserved.

Lying at the bottom of this hole in the dark, I made a decision. I wanted to be the type of person my daughter could be proud of. If I couldn't raise her, I would show her that I was someone who was capable of making more than naive choices.

I spent the next ten years striving for safe external goals: go to college, create a strong career, be active in my community. But emptiness punctuated my feelings. I navigated each relationship with reserve and arrested trust. I had lost my voice because secrets had paralyzed my self-esteem and, along with it, my authentic self-expression. Although my outward appearance was one of control and consistency, the emptiness inside became the eye of an emotional hurricane. My polished facade became a storm shelter. Forced into an existence of secrets, and silenced by external forces and the internal pressure to insulate myself, I pulled inward for self-comfort and protection.

During the decade before the truth would be revealed, I would lay awake at night wondering who I was, feeling lost at sea, drifting. I knew there would come a point when my daughter would come to me for answers. I knew that would be the hardest day I would ever face.

The Moment Illusions Shatter and Fear Must Be Met

A deep breath, and I stopped pacing and walked downstairs. My feet felt heavy in my shoes.

When I told my daughter the truth — that her mother was actually her grandmother and that I was her mother instead of her sister — illusions shattered like glass around us. We sat silent in my dining room, sharing individual tears, each of us with equal amounts of pain, but for very different reasons.

Later that evening she would tell me that she hadn't seen her adoption certificate in the photo album at her great grandma's house as was suspected; we had been mistaken about that.

I don't have room in this chapter to express the depth of heartache we endured or the joy we shared as we learned how to be together in a new way. Our story of reconnection will be told when I can write what must be gently said with enough words to fully express what we shared and how we learned to adjust to our sensitive hearts and live our new roles. I can tell you that in the chaos of learning that her world was not as it appeared to be, my daughter showed tremendous love for her family. Anger wasn't her response, although it easily could have been. Sorrow, however, entered her heart. Her faith in our family was shaken, and it took a few years of trial and tests to regain the trust she had so easily given to all of us before. The pendulum would swing from one side to the other as she would draw close and then retreat from all of us.

As the shock began to fade and the truth settled in, she became more comfortable within her identity and began to trust life once again. We began to see each other on deeper levels and eventually moved past the discomfort of constant emotional reminders.

Years passed and our spirits have settled, but to say the journey was easy or without struggle would not convey the texture of what we went through and what it took to get us where we are today. Time, consistency, forgiveness, and lots of unconditional love created the space for us to heal.

We laugh together, cry together, and make plans for the future we wish to share.

Untethered

In an area called your "Shadow" I learned to explore what my emotions felt but my mind repressed or disowned. Through layers of protection I was living with what I would later identify as self-induced amnesia. I wouldn't allow myself to think about what I was feeling; it simply was too scary to go there. This inner journey takes you into the dark to find what you deny yourself and, more important, what you must claim. Under the social mask and the layers of duty, I found the door that gave me not only access – call it an awareness, but also the ability to both see and heal what gave me emotional grief and inconsistent outcomes in my relationships.

A Look at My Blind Spots

The work on my Shadow guided me safely into a space from which I could witness the pain of my past. It taught me how to listen within; locate my true feelings; learn to be with discomfort, sorrow, and anger; and allow places for them in my consciousness. For the first time I felt the possibility of dominion over my emotions. I didn't have to hide from them or worry about their untimely eruptions. Feelings I had not been *able* to express, like anger and grief, were given a voice, and the ones I had *chosen* not to express, like passion and sensuality, started to bloom.

I was healing.

Aspects I had buried came to light, like my creativity in writing poetry. My essence started to show itself to me, and with it came a deep renewal of my spirit.

I found my disowned beauty and my bottled anger. I recognized how I had adapted myself to survive my circumstances, and had left my heart crying for attention. I made peace with each aspect and started creating a space for the parts of myself that needed a voice. I had to learn to honor what I couldn't be with.

I found my true self — a self that was not dictated by what the world wanted to see or by what I felt I needed to be in order to be accepted or, more important, loved.

My forgiveness didn't come with a flip of a switch, neither for myself nor for the others on this journey. It took time. Inner work has its own timing. It only takes a moment to change, but it can take a lifetime to get to that moment.

Everyone Carries a Shadow

In this life we are bombarded with opposing ideas about what we should do, be, or have. External voices clamor about what other people are or aren't, how we can be good in the eyes of others, and how we can be less bad in our own eyes. I cannot count how many personas I took on to navigate this world, but I now know intimately why they were born and how they served me, then and today.

Each persona protected my vulnerabilities, known or unknown to me. As I recognized this truth, I began to unplug from the competition within myself that all along I mistakenly believed came from my external environment. This act of seeing and learning to own all of me has become the work I do for others today.

Empathy for the souls and plights of others and the ability to see into sacrifices and fears are gifts that everyone possesses. I believe everyone has a story and wisdom to impart. In each conversation, we are both learning and teaching; we are all one step ahead or behind, being guided or led by those who share this world with us when we listen to each other.

Finding my voice again, I discovered a desire and passion to help others cope with struggles and move through higher levels of self-awareness so the peace we desire can be found.

Living with the loss or removal of a loved one, no matter what the cause, carries much weight in the heart. Even just the thought of it does, as you've seen here on these pages. But the loss of the relation and connection to self, our soul, conveys an equal burden.

My path through life has not been easy. I struggled with the pressures of teen pregnancy and the complex aftermath. Yet without that journey I wouldn't have come to know the richness of who my daughter and I are today as a result, nor would I be able to enrich other people's lives with the depth of my story.

One little girl learned she was a secret.

The other little girl learned she was, too.

Angela Hiroshima is a Shadow Path Facilitator and published author of a book being released in mid-2013. She is called "One who opens doorways to the mind and soul." Angela teaches and guides people to self-explore and find their voices and their power by removing the Shadow filters between the mind and spirit. She developed the Inner Evolution Course, a path through the Shadow. To discover more and receive a free Shadow Gift, visit www.AngelaHiroshima.com.

The Making of a Transformational Soul

Barbara Marx Hubbard

MANY, MANY YEARS AGO, I DECIDED ON THE simple act of writing down my daily thoughts in a plain, black, hard-bound journal. I had no idea that a shift in my consciousness would result from that simple decision.

I had a feeling that if I could describe the thoughts and feelings I was experiencing on those pages, they would become real in my world. I somehow knew that I was on a fundamental and spiritual path, yet I was uncertain about where this journey would take me.

I developed a technique of journal writing whereby I would ask a question and then turn off my "figuring-it-out mind" to allow my higher self to come through with responses. I'd then carefully write down the messages. Soon I learned about my own higher being and how to listen to what it was telling me.

Since I'm eighty-three years old, I'm one of the early birds of the transformational movement in the modern period. I must admit that at the beginning I had no idea what a transformational movement was, let alone where my transformation would take me in life! In that sense, I was a catalyst for the movement, and I also believe that I was the first to use a couple of the metaphors of transformation: "our crisis is a birth" and "evolution by choice not chance." From the thoughts in the 178 black, hard-bound journals I started at age eighteen, about seven books have been created.

I have been on a mission to communicate certain ideas about the positive future. I have used my written words and my speaking capability to attract people who were interested in the same shift of consciousness that I was, and who asked me to write books discussing this experience.

There are thousands of transformational leaders, visionaries, and people who have gone through amazingly difficult yet powerful and profound experiences who now want to bring their stories forward. They've made it their mission to put forth their positive message out into the world in the hopes of tipping the scales of humanity to the good.

Let me give you an example of how the written word is powerful in causing ripples of change: The words and records of what happened in early Greek and Roman times, and those of the early Christians and gospel writers, live on today. Empires may crumble and buildings may fall to ruins, but the written word does not. The words we hear and read can cause a shift in our thinking – our beliefs.

When I thought about the people who wrote the four books of the Gospel, I realized that they had a new "story to tell" that actually changed the world. I was inspired to ask the universe a great question: "What is our story to tell, that is as great as the story of the birth of Christ? A story that if we could tell it, would change the world." With that question, I had what I call a "planetary birth experience." I became like an astronaut seeing Earth as a living system from outer space – not just the globe in its geographic setting, but the Earth as a whole, struggling for survival. We were running out of energy and resources. I felt the pain of the whole social body within my own body. We felt all the pain of the world simultaneously, as the people of Earth. Then, I suddenly saw the Earth a few frames ahead into the future. I saw spirituality awaken from within in millions of us. Empathy increased and connected us through the heart. Healings occurred, and then I experienced all our social innovations as in health, energy, and economics connect like organs in the social body. I realized that we could actually make a "world that works for everyone," as Buckminster Fuller put it. In that one moment we had a shared experience of oneness, wholeness, goodness and creativity. Then I heard the words: "Our story is the birth of a universal humanity. Go tell the story, Barbara!"

After I wrote down this observation, I explored it in greater detail. I decided to study cosmology. I then went on to study biology and what humanity had really learned about this evolutionary universe story. The more I learned, the more I knew I had to tell others about how we are all interconnected, we are one, we are whole, we are being born toward a more co-creative species and a universal life in a universe of immeasurable dimensions. That led to my becoming a speaker about the story.

As I spoke, I wrote more in my journals, and gradually began to understand that my vision was accurate. I believe we are coming to the end of one phase of evolution. We are like a baby growing in the womb – it can't continue to live here indefinitely; it has to be born. We've been overgrowing in certain ways in the womb of Earth, destroying our environment and other species. That must stop! It will stop.

I began to see that our story is a new opening of evolution itself – evolution is becoming conscious through us. We are entering the first Age of Conscious Evolution. This means evolution by choice not chance. The deep intention of evolution itself – its divine intention

— is to create a species capable of consciously evolving. It's a huge breakthrough. We're the first species to realize that by our own acts we can destroy ourselves. Crises like the ones we are going through now are evolutionary drivers; either we evolve or we face extinction. Only through our own acts can we evolve ourselves.

My book *Birth 2012 and Beyond:Humanity's Great Shift to the Age of Conscious Evolution* is a manual of how to participate in our society's rebirth. I call it a "map to cross the gap." The purpose is to bridge the gap between the Earth's breakdowns and its breakthrough.

There are certain practices that really help us become "agents of conscious evolution." One has to gain evolutionary eyes to see that our crisis can be a birth — that's our number one step forward... a new sense of meaning, hope, and direction to our lives. Number two is to put yourself in the evolutionary story as an expression of the process of creation internalized within you. When you place yourself within the evolutionary spiral, you feel the impulse inside of you to change; it's an evolutionary impulse. You are turned on. Then you can practice what is called "heart math," through which you begin to feel your heart and your love deepen and you experience resonance between your heart, your brain, and others in society. That resonance helps you shift your sense of identity to your own essence, your own true nature. Then you reach out to others. You find your neighbors and bring them together. You are stimulated to find your deeper life purpose, to co-create with others, to fulfill your soul's code in spirit-motivated evolutionary action. You become a participant in the on-going planetary birthing process. You become a pioneering soul, part of a movement for the conscious evolution of humanity.

When any one of us fully expresses our deeper self and our life purpose, we're serving the world and serving ourselves at the same time. We are helping each other shift from our egoist, separated selves to more connected, cooperative selves. Many of us are becoming a new type of human, which I call "universal human." This is a person who feels connected through the heart to the whole of life; who is awakened from within by a spiritual impulse to give more, to be more. We become co-creators with the greater process of creation itself.

"Our crisis can be a birth." This is what we were born for. Just that one phrase makes such a difference. There is an evolutionary calling within this universal human, a sensitivity to what's emerging and what's new and creative. We realize that we are an evolving humanity. People who feel this are the pioneers of the next stage of evolution.

Tapping the Source from within – the desire to express and create – applies to all writers. At eighty-three I'm feeling regenerated by this Impulse of Evolution. In my teaching, in my Agents of Conscious Evolution training (ACE) I'm calling for people who want to evolve, to become connected to their own hearts, then to shift from ego to essence, to become their own true nature. Then comes "vocational arousal," discovering our deeper life purpose, seeking out new partners and teams, becoming co-creators of our own lives and the world.

Individually and collectively we're at a tipping point in human history. The system can break down… or break through. What tips us in a positive direction is human thought and human creativity. Writers who are infusing our collective consciousness with transformation, caring, and inspiration are actually contributing to the planetary shift. They really help us see that we are all part of the movement.

What I mean by *movement* is the combined action of countless individuals, awakening to their heart's desire to participate more deeply in self and social evolution by finding their true nature and calling, and acting in the world. I'm fond of saying to all visionaries, "Don't die!" Just stay alive. Because if you stay alive long enough, saying YES to your own love and creativity, you will be participating in the evolution of yourself and the world. There is no greater opportunity.

My whole life has been focused on writing, speaking, and evolutionary activism. Active writing is one of the greatest services we can offer to our evolution and that of our culture. It comes from within you. The more you can articulate it, the more real it becomes in your own life and the lives of others.

When your words come from the very essence of your being, you are giving your gift to the whole world.

Barbara Marx Hubbard has been called "the voice for conscious evolution of our time" by Deepak Chopra and is the subject of Neale Donald Walsch's new book *"The Mother of Invention."* A prolific author, visionary, social innovator, evolutionary thinker, and educator, she is co-founder and chairperson of the Foundation for Conscious Evolution. She is the producer and narrator of the award-winning documentary series entitled *Humanity Ascending: A New Way Through Together* and is teaching her seminal course: Agents of Conscious Evolution with The Shift Network, becoming a global ambassador for the conscious evolution movement; a shift from evolution by chance towards evolution by choice. www.BarbaraMarxHubbard.com

Transform Your Trauma into Your Triumph

Calli D. Meister

TO MY SURPRISE THE CAR KEY WOULD NOT slip into the door lock.

Bang! A violent blast deafened my ears and knocked me to the ground. I lay there on the cold, concrete floor of the parking garage, unable to move my legs. Thousands of thoughts converged into one microsecond. *What's happening? Why can't I feel my legs? Why are they shaking?* Looking over my shoulder, I saw him. Our eyes met and horror filled my veins. My ex-boyfriend, Jay, stood just a few feet behind me holding two rifles, one under each arm. Confused and terrified, I asked, "Did you shoot me?"

Wearing cowboy boots and a leather jacket, his six-foot-three frame silently towered over me. Trembling, I asked, "Why did you shoot me, Jay?" I frantically ran my hands down my right leg, then my left, feeling for wounds.

"If I can't have you, no one can!" Jay's gruff, booming voice echoed off the cars and walls in the parking garage. "Look at me!" he insisted, as he aimed the barrel of one rifle directly at my head. "Look at me!" I froze... couldn't breathe... couldn't think. "TELL ME WHY

I SHOULDN'T KILL YOU RIGHT NOW!" he demanded with his finger on the trigger.

How should I answer him? What will stop him? He's about to pull the trigger again! Suddenly the memory of my mother's instruction to "never stare down an angry dog" flashed through my mind. I looked away from Jay's penetrating eyes, not wanting to provoke him. "No, Jay, don't!" I pleaded. "You love me. You don't want to do this! Please, Jay, stop!"

Attempting to gain protection under my car, I pulled myself forward. I found none. To my dismay the undercarriage of my compact two-door was too low for my head to fit under. Determined to escape, I crawled arm over arm towards the front bumper and the garage wall. Continuing to point the barrel at me, Jay followed my every move as I slowly dragged my unresponsive legs across the garage floor.

I have to get away! I have been through so much already! I have so many dreams to fulfill!

"LOOK AT ME!" Jay's voice suddenly exploded again. "LOOK AT ME RIGHT NOW!" Obediently I jerked my head around as ordered, praying Jay's face would not be the last thing I ever saw. "No one will want you the way you are now! This is all your fault! You are to blame!" Jay's angry voice screamed "LOOK AT ME!" Abruptly he pivoted the rifle, pointing it under his own chin.

"No, Jay, don't!" I cried out. "I love you! I really do love you! You need help, that's all! You just need help! Please! Don't do this! Please don't kill yourself! Go, now! I won't tell anyone! Just go!" I pleaded.

Jay blasted, "If I let *you* live, I'm not going to leave you with anyone else to love!" before bolting out of the parking garage and disappearing into the darkness. I listened to each pounding boot step fade as the distance grew between us.

I knew instantly he meant he was going to kill the people I loved! Frantic, I scanned the ground for my car keys and located them under the passenger side of the car. Driven to warn my family, I dragged myself closer and stretched under the car to reclaim the keys. I reached up to the door handle and slipped the key into place. Just as I heard the door unlock, the garage filled with brilliant light. Headlights! Someone was coming! Help was here!

A female driver was at the wheel. Her wiper blades swished the rain from her windshield. Our eyes met as she stopped the vehicle. "HELP ME!" I shouted. Her eyes looked away to scan the garage. She spotted the rifle Jay had laid on the floor. That was the turning point for her. The car backed away and out of the underground garage. "WAIT!" I yelled. "COME BACK! I NEED HELP!"

How could she leave? Oh, God, please give me strength!

I yanked at the door's handle until the door opened. I lifted my body up and across the front seats. I inserted the key in the ignition and started the engine.

"Dear God, help me. HELP ME!" I prayed. Lying across the front seat and below the steering wheel, I put one hand to the gas pedal and the other on the wheel. From this vantage point, my only guide was the ceiling of the garage, which I could barely see through the portion of window above the dashboard.

Inch by inch, I escaped the scene of horror as I drove my car with my hands.

Alternating from the brake pedal to the gas, I made it out into the street. I strained to pull myself upright into the driver's position and leaned on the horn. I screamed out the window, "PLEASE! SOMEBODY HELP ME!" Lights flashed in the distance, making their way towards me! Tears streamed over my cheeks. Within seconds the paramedics were instructing me to unlock my front door.

"You need to call my mother!" I screamed. "You've got to warn my family! Hurry! He's going to kill my family! They're in Cloverdale! Please, you've got to warn them!"

"Miss, you're injured. We're here to help *you*!" the medic said.

"I'm not going *anywhere* until you send them help!" I insisted. "I won't let you touch me until you do!" My panic was relieved when the medic reached for his radio and I heard him call in my information to the authorities.

I released the door lock. The paramedic cautiously laid me over the steering wheel as another flashed a bright light into my car. My clothing was cut away, layer by layer, and there it was... a bullet hole in my back. I had been shot. No exit wound was found. An overwhelming feeling that I might not survive swelled over me as I was lifted into the ambulance. I looked up into the warm eyes of the paramedic and asked, "Would you hold my hand please... in case I die before I make it to the hospital?"

He gripped my hand firmly, looked straight into my eyes, and flatly stated, "You are going to live, my dear." With those words of encouragement, I experienced a comforting wave of peace wash over my body.

Upon arrival at the hospital emergency room, I was examined by the doctor and a portable x-ray machine was rushed to my bedside. Just then my mother and stepfather arrived, without my sister. "Mom, where's Chanty?!" I demanded.

"Your sister is at work, sweetheart, no need to worry," my mother reported, quivering with emotion.

Dr. Bright Eyes, as I remember him, interrupted us. "I have good news! Look at this x-ray!" he began. "The bullet is lodged in your spine and has cut one of your main cords."

Where is the good news in this? I wondered. The doctor continued, "The nerve is cut. However, it is not entirely severed. A few thin fibers remain intact and the best course of action is to leave the bullet in place. Removing the bullet guarantees paralysis; leaving it in place offers a glimmer of hope."

In that instant I clung to the shred of hope he offered. The vision of walking, running, and dancing again was the life I was choosing. I was only twenty years old and earlier that day I had received my acceptance letter for the new semester of college. I had just begun to live my life!

I was whisked up to a private room and a guard stood outside my door. The nurse told me she was giving me something to help me rest, but I didn't expect to be sedated for several days. Upon waking three days later, I questioned what had happened and the nurse explained they had knocked me out to aid my body in recovering from the trauma.

The back pain came on strong as the medications wore off. I was committed to taking as few drugs as possible. I did not like the way the medication made my brain foggy. I had my mind made up to fully heal and return to all the activities I loved, and the physical limitations were not going to stop me.

The extraordinary athletic coaches I'd had during my childhood had instilled in me the benefits of determination and visualization. The moment that smiling-eyed doctor offered me my shred of hope, I claimed it as my destiny. I meditated on my strong, vibrant body returning to perfect health! Spirit over matter, I was determined to walk again!

My legs remained numb, yet I understood my mission: to get my feet and legs moving again as soon as possible. I called upon the teachings of my basketball coaches who taught me to visualize the ball in the net *before* the ball left my hands. I started with bed exercises, learning to move my listless legs and feet.

My devoted mother faithfully stayed at my bedside. We bonded in new and heightened ways. We shared positive visions of the future. During our special time together she reminded me of a favored bedtime story from my childhood: *The Little Engine That Could*. I reacquainted myself with the empowering concept and began to say mantras to the familiar tune. "I know I can! I know I can! I am strong! I am strong!"

115

Within one week I was standing, though I was held by supportive therapists as I teetered on my legs. The following week I advanced to using a walker with assistance. I would swing one foot in front of the other by using my hips as swivels, all the while visualizing my legs strong and moving fluidly again. Each day I was getting stronger. I was ecstatic when I graduated to walker-walking without assistance, and started doing laps up and down the hospital hall. I would set my goals a little farther each day, and thrived on the encouragement from my mother, visitors, nurses, and caregivers.

Even though I was physically mobile using the walker, I only had about fifty percent of the feeling in my legs. The doctors could not assure me as to how much mobility would return to my lower extremities, yet all agreed they were surprised by my success thus far. In three short weeks I was ready to leave the hospital and continue my physical therapy on my own.

"Sweetheart," my mother announced one morning, "I want you to stay with us during your recovery. To be sure you're safe and cared for... taking the prescriptions... eating well."

Us? I thought. *You want me to go back into the silence of our family secrets and forget about all the abuse there? Home with you and Chanty, yes... but home with him? My stepfather? I would rather not subject myself to his rampages again.*

"Okay, Mom, I'll come to your house because I would love your help. It's the best option as I don't want to be alone right now. However, no prescriptions; I want to remain clear-minded and stable on my feet. I'll heal much faster that way."

Once in the house, I began a rigorous self-healing routine of physiotherapy sessions and home exercises during which I pushed past the pain with my sights on my goal. I visualized myself walking the white, sandy beaches of Hawaii and body-surfing the waves that set me free. Motivated by a deep, inner strength stronger than my limitations, I pushed myself harder with each passing week and emerged one Sunday morning, dressed and ready to reconnect with friends in the congregational community.

I pushed my walker through the doorway and onto the porch. Invigorating, brisk air filled my lungs and rejuvenated my senses. I felt wonderful being alive! *One step at a time,* I reminded myself. *I know I can, I am strong.* As I slid my walker inches forward, a sharp, sudden bolt of energy jolted down my legs. *My legs! My legs! Oh, my God, I feel my legs and feet!* "MOM, LOOK," I proclaimed, "Look, I am walking!" I stepped away from the walker, threw up my hands, and gave thanks.

By Monday morning I was on the phone planning the details of my trip to Hawaii. A few weeks later I was there, in Honolulu. I arrived alive and walking! I filled my days and evenings with nature, swimming in the ocean, soaking up the sun, hula dance classes, and enjoying the life I had envisioned in my mind.

Only three short months after the shooting, on my twenty-first birthday, I was experiencing and living in paradise. I was the miracle of my own making. That day I set my intention. No more reliving the details of my nightmare with Jay; no more allowing people to feel sorry for me. I wanted the shooting behind me, and right then vowed to myself not to reveal my past to anyone in my future.

Since then I've dedicated my life to continue learning and sharing the empowerment and healing tools most helpful to me during my recovery. I became a sought-after holistic healer, wellness consultant, and life coach, and enjoyed empowering individuals, corporations, and celebrities, all the while keeping my own ordeal private.

Twenty years later, however, in May of 2011, I was awakened in my sleep by what can only be described as a divine voice – a profound and clear command telling me, "Calli, the world needs to hear your story. You need to share it!" Simultaneously a movie appeared in my vision that allowed me to witness my story, now played by actors, for the benefit of others.

We all have within us the strength to create miraculous lives, *if* we choose to. Your beliefs, Your commitment, and Your Spirit are here to empower you to triumph over the trauma in *your* life! Connect with and command the strength of Spirit within yourself.

Calli Meister has impacted the lives of tens of thousands as a trusted Wellness Consultant, Master Intuitive Energy Practitioner, and Spiritual Guide. Through her powerful journey from abuse and paralysis to standing triumphant, Calli is living proof of the strength within the steadfast Spirit. She now shares her extraordinary story globally, empowering others as a transformational energy healer, intuitive life coach, retreat facilitator, author, and powerhouse speaker. Learn more and receive Calli's free audio meditation, "The Self Empowerment Key" at www.CalliMeister.com.

From Devastation to Celebration!

Fiona Miller, BSc

AT THE HEART OF EVERY SEEMINGLY disastrous or devastating event there is a seed of transformation — a seed that if found can have a transformational effect on your life and, because we are all energetically interconnected, the lives of others.

I have noticed this countless times, especially during the past two years when two unexpected, unwelcome events turned my life upside down and gave me a great opportunity to dive within and find rich treasure.

It was almost daybreak when, on September 4th, 2010, I woke suddenly. My bed was rolling violently and things were falling to the floor all around me. It was dark — pitch black. Without any warning Mother Earth was being wrenched apart, fractured; she was releasing vast amounts of energy right under my bed... my home... my city!

I lay there motionless, somewhat stunned. Then, almost instinctively, I connected to Spirit and felt a deep sense of peace... as if I was being looked after. In that moment I knew I was going to be alright. After thirty seconds the rolling stopped. I got out of bed and hesitantly went down the stairs. What was I going to see? What exactly had happened? What devastation was going to greet me?

I carefully stepped over broken crockery and fallen treasures. Pictures on the walls hung askew, clear evidence of the violence of the quake. Dazed neighbors in their nightgowns knocked on our door. Were we okay?

As dawn broke, the full extent of the quake became visible: land torn apart, the sea-wall opposite our home broken, neighbors' buildings no longer on their foundations, and miniature volcanoes of silt forced up through fissures in the road and park.

That night of the earthquake I learned that everything, except for my connection to Spirit, can disappear or change radically in a moment. I learned the immense value of being connected to Spirit. I transformed an intellectual belief that Spirit is constantly present into a heart-felt *knowing* that Spirit is present. I quickly appreciated what I did value: my relationships and my connection to others, including Spirit. I became truly grateful for what I had in that moment.

In the early days after the earthquake there was scarcely an hour that went by without a tremor. I promptly learned to stay in the present and stop my creative mind from focusing on the future and what might happen.

In the weeks and months that followed, Mother Earth continued to shake violently, releasing vast amounts of energy and realignment. What was Mother Earth telling me and humanity? What energy did I and humanity need to release? What realignment did I and humanity need to make?

Considering these questions I realized that the time to release fears, to realign and connect with Spirit was *now*, not sometime in the future. *Now* was the time to trust Spirit and heed my calling – what my heart yearned for. *Now* was the time to be in my Truth.

In the twelve months that followed, I became more aligned with my Truth and deepened my connection to Spirit. I paid more attention to

Spirit's message, trusted it more, and took inspired action. Guided by Spirit, I started to write a book to support readers in their alignment with their Truths and the high vibrations of joy, peace, and fulfillment.

During this transformative time I became more comfortable with my relationship with Spirit. I also became concerned about times when I succumbed to old behaviors and beliefs. I was reactive rather than proactive, and found myself in the low vibrations of frustration and, at times, powerlessness. Because I was questioning my ability to be more powerful and manage my energy more effectively, I did not complete the book before going on vacation as planned. Deep down I felt that I had to receive another message from Spirit before I could complete it. It was with this in mind that I left for Italy, a place I had always longed to visit.

One week into our holiday, my partner and I were in Naples in the south of Italy. While there, we had two destinations in mind: Mount Vesuvius and the Royal Palace of Caserta. It was a beautiful day in May and we decided that it was the perfect day for a visit to the Palace. Getting there involved a short train trip out of Naples, an adventure and an opportunity to see more of the countryside. Our plans during the previous twenty-four hours had gone wrong several times, and as we left the bustle of Naples we looked forward to a relaxing visit to the Palace.

On our arrival we paid our entrance fee and then, to our dismay, were told that there would be no English-speaking guides until the afternoon. We were deeply disappointed. Once again our plans had been thwarted. After a short discussion we decided on an alternative plan: to hire bikes and tour the extensive grounds of the Palace. As we cycled through the formal grounds, past the pools, fountains, and sculptures, I felt both frustrated and powerless. How could everything go so wrong? Then, as if we had not had enough challenges that day, the sky darkened and the heavens opened. Within moments we were soaked to the skin.

Hastily we put on our jackets and made the decision to cycle back downhill to the shelter of the Palace. My partner set off first and as he headed downhill I heard him call out, "Let's go!" I followed. My head was down trying to shelter my eyes from the full impact of the rain which was trickling down the back of my neck. Thump! My bike hit a pothole and before I knew it I was lying on the ground!

I'm told it was thirty minutes before the ambulance came. I remember very little, only the comforting thought that I was going to be alright. It was like that night of the earthquake. I felt deep peace, as if I was being looked after.

The hours in the hospital were grim. I was alone in the accident waiting room, wet, cold, and aching. No one seemed to understand or speak English. Injured patients came and went. When was someone going to attend to me? Eventually x-rays were taken. Then, after six hours of discomfort, the doctor appeared and told me that I had broken my collarbone and shoulder blade, and the best thing I could do was "go home." I was devastated but took his advice and we arranged our immediate return home to New Zealand.

In the weeks that followed, I spent sleepless nights sitting upright, and my mind began to play tricks with me. It was easy to imagine future disastrous scenarios. Then I was reminded of the lessons that followed the earthquake and began to seriously practice staying present and connected to Spirit. In doing so I found much comfort and lots to be grateful for, and within weeks I strengthened my *knowing* about being present and connected to Spirit.

As I waited for a surgery date, hearing nothing from my doctors, my gratitude and patience were tested. My collarbone looked increasingly out of alignment but I appeared to be the only one who was concerned. For eight weeks prior to surgery my arm was strapped to my body to immobilize my shoulder and reduce further misalignment of my collarbone. During this stressful time I felt frustrated and began to blame others for my situation. How could the wheels of bureaucracy turn so slowly?

As the dis-ease continued, I passively accepted my situation and the low-vibration energies of powerlessness, fear, frustration, blame, pessimism, and self-criticism. I was acting as if my energy state was the responsibility of others — as if it was in the hands of others. Only when I realized this did I actively start to be self-responsible, choose my energy state, and set positive intentions. I released the low-vibration energies, connected to Spirit, opened my heart, and welcomed into my life the higher vibrations of joy, peace, and love. By actively managing my energy I discovered how much more powerful I felt and how much happier I could be even when I was in ill health.

Recovering from my accident took over five months, and during this time I was forced to slow down. As a life-long over achiever, this was something I had always been loath to do. I learned, however, that being my true Self was possible, even when I was not running around "doing" or "achieving" — that there was no need to be a slave to my ego mind. Furthermore I discovered that I could embrace my presence — my "being" in Truth and my "being" in Love and Light — much more easily when my ego mind was quieted and not telling me what I "should" or "must" do. I discovered that I could live in my heart, and embrace my presence — my "being" in Truth, and my "being" in Love and Light — much more easily when my ego mind was quieted and not telling me what I "should" or "must" do.

As I continued to question my accident and why it had happened, I came to realize that my plan was not necessarily Spirit's plan.

Surrendering to Spirit's plan rather than fighting it was the better option, one that had a vital message for me and would be more rewarding and transformational in the long term.

Today in my life and business I *know* that Spirit is the source of power. I *know* that by listening to my heart rather than my ego, asking for guidance, and allowing the high-frequency energies of Spirit to flow through me I am able to be in my power, co-create, and manifest powerful outcomes. If my accident hadn't taught me to actively manage my energy and open my heart to Spirit, I know that this would not have happened. I would still be experiencing the once-familiar low vibrations of frustration and powerlessness.

Thankfully the question I was asking myself before I went to Italy has now been answered. I have learned valuable lessons about managing my energy more effectively and being more powerful. Consequently I am now able to complete the writing of my book *Taps on the Shoulder — How to Transform Unwelcome Life Events Into Your Greatest Gifts.*

The earthquakes and the accident were devastating on one level, yet at a deeper level I know they were invaluable, transformational, and cause for celebration. When I ask myself what my life has taught me over the past two years, I can confidently say that these two events strengthened my alignment and deepened my connection to Spirit; taught me to actively manage my energy; tamed my achiever, ego-centered Self; opened my heart to more loving, peaceful, and joyful energy; and caused me to take action to create more meaning and celebration in my life. They have shifted me from an intellectual belief in connection to Spirit to a heart-felt knowing that I am at one with Spirit.

I connect to Spirit daily, ask for guidance, and follow it knowing that if I do not I will have regrets. I more readily honor my divine Self and find myself more willing to step into my power with joy — to radiantly shine from within and be visible from afar.

Everything in this Universe is energetically connected; we all affect each other. No one is in isolation. Each one of us can receive high-vibration energies including love, joy, and peace. These energies are there for us if we are willing to open our hearts, connect with Spirit and receive them.

Knowing this, I now feel called to share the insights that I received from these seemingly devastating events in my life. In doing so I hope that you, too, will find the gift in your seemingly devastating events and experience a greater alignment and deeper connection to Spirit. May you, too, raise your vibration and bring joy, love, and inner peace to your Self and humanity.

Fiona Miller, BSc started her professional life as an ecologist in the seventies. Then as a certified counselor, teacher and coach she worked in the field of personal and professional development for over twenty years. Today Fiona is a spiritual teacher, mentor, and author. She inspires others to positively contribute to the future well-being of humanity and Mother Earth by living from their hearts rather than their heads. For additional information, visit www. TapsOnTheShoulder.com.

Paving the Path to Transformation

Lisa Nichols

I WAS BORN AND RAISED IN SOUTH CENTRAL, Los Angeles, and lived between the "Harlem Crip 30's" and "The Rollin' 60's." I say all the time, those are not cheerleading squads – those are gangs! I had, on average, three fights a week on my way home from school. Some people tell me that my life was so insane and crazy, but the funny thing is I didn't know it was challenging at the time. It was just my life. As it was the norm for me, I didn't know that it was challenging until I got out of it, took my first breath, and realized, "Oh my God. I've been holding my breath for eighteen years."

I was an average C student. I'd literally struggled in almost every single course. I later learned that I'm a kinesthetic learner – a tactile learner, so the school system was very, very difficult for me to get through. The last time I took an English course, I received a fail and my English teacher said in front of the entire class, "Lisa, you have to be the weakest writer I've ever met in my entire life." That same year I took my first and last speech class and my speech teacher gave me a D and said, "Miss Nichols, I recommend you never speak in public." But, you know what I realized? That some motivation comes wrapped in sandpaper. If you think about some of the things that have inspired you to keep going the most, they weren't covered with glittering gold and hearts, all warm and fuzzy. So instead of having inspirational motivation, I had a little bit of "I'll show you" motivation.

Things happen, but if you can re-purpose them to serve as your fuel, not your fortress, between you and your goal, and let them not be your reason for not trying or succeeding, then you can change any situation. That's what I did. I put a placeholder in my life and said, "Listen, this was the first six chapters of my life, but the next six chapters are blank sheets of paper. I hold the pen in my hand and either I can copy and paste the old story into a new chapter, or I can rewrite or write for the first time a new experience." And that's what I chose to do.

There is no sprinkle of fairy dust, no magic potion lotion, no wand, nothing that was waved over my life that instantly changed it and all my bad experiences suddenly became good. There wasn't any one moment when the heavens opened up and a bright light came down to me and I was a new person. That wasn't my experience. My awakening was very practical. I was so sick and tired of being only a portion of my greatness that it became more painful for me to live in this false sense of safety than it was frightening for me to stand up and step into a new possibility.

I want you to know that in my small world, I was already earning six figures by the time I was thirty-five. I was literally one of the most sought after people in Los Angeles to get things done throughout the community, both with the legislature and our local government. So in my small world, I had a "big title," but I knew that I held this title only in Los Angeles when I received my calling. God was telling me to serve the Universe: the planet and humanity, not just South Central or Los Angeles, not even Southern California. For me, it was a very practical experience; it was my everyday life. I knew that for every day that passed when I didn't tell my story, when I didn't step up on my platform, when I didn't push past my fear storms, a piece of my own possibility was dying away. I knew that I didn't want to get old and sit in my rocking chair and have a story of "I could've, I would've, I should've, but I didn't." My transformation was an "I was so inspired" type of revelation. It was a, "Wait a minute. I know there's a greatness in me. I know there's a goodness in me. I was given a gift and I'd better share it with the world because it wasn't given to me to hold to myself."

I had to push past my own fear storms. I was afraid of being judged. I didn't graduate from college, and was afraid that I wasn't smart enough. I'm an African-American woman. I have full lips, round hips, and kinky hair. I didn't look like a supermodel. I had all this chatter in my head about why I shouldn't take the leap, but I had this burning in my belly that was bigger and greater than any conversation going on in my mind. And it kept me up at nights, wondering what was possible in my life. Until finally, I said, "I'm going to take the leap, because I'd rather fall trying than stay safe and never have risked anything and live in this small perception of success, this appeared victory."

An appeared victory is when the cost of the success outweighs the success itself and it's a false victory. I wanted to really see what it felt like. I have to tell you, nothing in my physical plane, not family, not finances, not that I was a single mother when I started (I had a three-year-old son when I took this leap) — nothing in my physical plane was in alignment and said, "This is what you should do." But my GPS system, or my God Placement System as I call it, screamed so loudly to who I could become if I had faith and if I understood that my path does not, in any shape or form, equal my future, said I could take that leap. And I did.

I began a journey that I've called "Paving the path to transformation." I want each of you to truly understand what that means. It doesn't mean I'm going to walk the path or follow the one already created. It means I'm going to pave the path. Let's define this. Paving the path is having your elbows up, chin down, pushing your way forward. It may seem at times that you have cement stuck on your elbows and hands, and your back is tired from doing the work. It means that when you walk and you make that path, you're going to have bruises on your body from all that hard work.

I remember at nineteen asking my professor, "Why is college so hard for me? Does God have a plan for me?" I mean, God had his hand on my life at age nineteen. And I remember complaining once to this professor because I was always the only person of color in every environment I was in. I usually had to do the whole humanity conversation about what it felt like to be black and to be in my skin. At this particular age I said, "God, why do I have to always be the person to explain this to everyone?" And very quickly God said, "I'm using you. You are my instrument." When my professor replied, he said, "Because you're paving the path. You have bruises on your forehead, nose, and your chin because you're not walking down a road created; you're creating the road in the woods. The bushes are going to hit your face first, but someone's going to come behind you who won't have to have that discomfort because you took it on. That's your role. That's your assignment." So when you say pave the path of transformation, you have to understand what pave means. It means that you're the creator – like Michelangelo created the sculpture *David*.

Transformation is neither fast nor convenient. My grandmother said, "Your convictions will never be convenient, so be worthwhile and worthy of a lifetime of service." Transformation is not something you can do a Google download and get. While it's necessary and life-giving, when you're paving a path for transformation, you're doing two incredible things simultaneously. Your soul has already said yes and now you just have to get your mind, mouth, and your action congruent with your soul so that you can live in your highest purpose.

Please do not wait to stop feeling the fear and take the leap. If I had waited, I would still be sitting on the edge of the cliff going, "Well, when my son gets out of school..." or "When I lose a little more weight..." because I'm a "run-on sentence" Mom. I don't put the period in until I finish my thought. Believe me, if I waited until I could distinguish between a semicolon and a colon and where each one was supposed to go, you would not have any books from me right now. You would not hear me at speaking engagements right now. So my first very practical advice to you would be to become committed and not wait to make a change until the fear is gone.

Determination is looking in the face of your fear and moving anyway. You don't have to be without fear to take the leap. Breathe that in. You don't have to wait until you're feeling totally courageous to take the leap. You can take the leap still feeling a bit uncertain. That's where faith steps in. See, faith is the evidence of the unseen, knowing that the unseen will take place. So take the leap in the face of fear because then that proves your determination. Be sure that when you take that leap, one of three things will happen (and this is my belief system in action). When you take the leap off the ledge, either the universe will give you wings to fly, you'll get something soft to land on, or you'll get a great big Band-Aid if you fall. I've gotten all three and I'm okay. No worries. Take that leap.

The second exercise in undergoing your transformation is to recognize your chatter and accept it for what it is. I do this exercise in my book *No Matter What* called "Expose the lie." It's one of the most powerful exercises I've ever done for myself which is why I put it in the first chapter of my book. I know that this is true for so many people. We all have a compulsive voice in our heads, and sometimes it's a full-blown committee. Some days we have the entire cellular network in our head telling us who we can't be or what we can't do. To minimize how important those voices are to your life, I'm not going to ever tell you that you can silence that chatter. I'm going to tell you how you can minimize and manage the chatter because I haven't had a day or a month or a period of time in my life when I didn't have that negative talk going on. I just learned how to masterfully manage my negative chatter.

Here's the micro-version of how to "Expose the lie." Get at least ten sheets of paper, a pencil, and a red pen. In pencil, I want you to expose every lie that you say about yourself. Don't limit it just to your writing or speaking ability. Write about your health, relationships, finances, your spirituality — talk about everything. Now write down one lie at a time, skip four lines, write the next one down and so on. Why do you have ten sheets of paper? Because the bigger you play in the world, the more lies you'll have to expose. If you're playing big in the world, you're going to have breakdowns, and if you don't have breakdowns, you're not playing big enough. Negative chatter comes with breakdowns and playing big. You'll want to write down all your lies and dump them. It might take you several hours and you may want to do it over a period of a few days, but don't walk away from this exercise until you feel like you've dumped everything out.

Now that you have all the lies dumped out in pencil, in between each lie in the spaces I want you to grab the red pen and write the truth. This is where you're going to get stuck. You may say, "I don't know what the truth is," and I'm going to respond by saying, "In this moment, you know that there has to be a corresponding truth because you've identified the lie." You may not be able to believe the truth right now and that's totally fine. Neuro Linguistic Programming (NLP) says, "Put the truth there so that you can see it, so that when you are ready to believe it, you have access to it." At this stage you'll have the lie in pencil and the truth in red ink. Next I want you to read the lie and the truth for two days. What we're creating is a counterbalance. In the future, when you think of the lie, you automatically see the truth in red ink. After you read the lie and the truth for two days, then I want you to erase everything in pencil, which happens to be all the lies. And the only thing you'll be left with is the truth.

Are you willing at the end of reading this chapter, right now in this moment, to follow your true calling? If you are, declare it. Have a breakthrough out loud. Don't make it a quiet breakthrough. When you breakthrough out loud, your energy becomes contagious to other people. Stand up and say out loud, "Oh, by the way, I just decided to become non-negotiable. I realized it was optional yesterday. Today it's non-negotiable." That's when you start moving out of your way and big things will happen in your life.

Follow your calling. It's the only way to fulfill your true purpose on this earth and bring you happiness in your life.

Lisa Nichols is a best-selling author, a popular public speaker, a powerful coach, and a charismatic teacher! She has reached millions, both nationally and internationally, with her powerful message of empowerment, service, excellence, and gratitude. Her participation in the self-development phenomenon, *The Secret*, catapulted her popularity across the globe. Lisa has appeared on the *Oprah Winfrey Show*, *Extra*, *Larry King Live*, and on NBC's Emmy Award-winning show, *Starting Over*. Her book, *No Matter What!* hit six bestsellers lists, including the *New York Times*, in the first thirty-seven days of being released. www.Lisa-Nichols.com

Wake Up, Sleeping Beauty

Rosie Quigley

"YOU RAISE ME UP, so I can stand on mountains. You raise me up, to walk on stormy seas. I am strong when I am on your shoulders. You raise me up to be more than I can be." An angel named Celine is singing this song to me and I feel wrapped in the arms of love. She supports me and is helping me write this story.

I have discovered from talking to hundreds of people that humanity is experiencing a crisis in which most people feel they are not receiving enough encouragement. Many are quick to criticize. Having the ability to speak sweet, kind words to yourself enables you to feel more supported in life.

What if you felt more encouraged? Then you could make positive changes. What if your negative self-talk became... sweet and kind? Then perhaps you could dwell in possibilities and feel happier.

Perhaps you are like me and have rarely heard, "You are beautiful." For most of my life I hadn't heard these sweet words. Instead I heard, "I'm glad you are not beautiful. Beautiful women lead painful lives."

Hearing Angel Celine say, "Rosie, you are lovely," I discovered it to be true. As I changed my thinking, I became sparkly, inside and

135

out. Taking Angel Celine as your guide, she will help you feel more confident, beautiful, and sparkly, too.

Growing up Catholic, I knew about angels, yet they were not part of my everyday life. Celine came to me three years ago during a long, sad time. I had been confined to my home, ill for over sixteen years, and wasn't able to bear a child. She became my best friend and gave me hope for a brighter future.

The Happy Beginning

It was June of 2009 and I was feeling much emotional pain. I had just completed a three-month treatment for Lyme disease and had hoped I would be well as summer began. Instead my symptoms worsened and I felt worse. After many years of living with an illness that kept me confined to my home, I felt despair. Doctor after doctor said, "You are the sickest person I have ever treated and I don't know how to help you." Their help only set me back. Not knowing what else to do, I turned to God and prayer. Carefully I followed the guidance I received.

After weeks of praying for relief, I listened to a talk by Gary Reynard at Sounds True about surrender. I decided to give up control and said, "God, you are in charge of my health, my relationship, my finances, everything." I let go of my timeline for finding solutions and getting well.

Ten days later I woke with a migraine headache, feeling surrounded by "brain fog" and crying. My neighbor had painted one side of his house and the wind had shifted, causing the paint smells to enter our home. Over the next two months seven structures were painted within one block of our home. Even with an air filter running full time, our home ended up smelling like a paint factory. I could not remain in our house, so I sought refuge in the forest down the road. My husband took the seats out of our old mini-van so I could lie down in the back of the car and this became my new home. Often when I returned to our house, I ended up in a confrontation with my husband who insisted, "I can't smell any paint."

All the stress was depleting me. One day returning to the forest, I felt a magnetic pull towards a large, white, umbrella-shaped flower called cow parsnip. I asked the flower's permission to pick it. Resting in the warm sun along the river's edge, surrounded by ancient Sitka spruce trees, I placed the flower on my heart and prayed for healing.

Energy entered the soles of my feet and traveled up my body. As my body calmed, my muscles let go and peace enfolded me. Over the past year I had become magnetically attracted to particular plants, depending on my need at the moment. Each plant has a unique healing gift, and I often think of them as Earth angels. Upon receiving permission to pick the flower, I'd place it on my heart to receive its healing gift.

After living in the forest for a couple of weeks, one morning, I wondered when I would return home. I felt despair. Sitting among the Shasta daisies, an insight came. My inner victim said, "Poor me. Ain't this awful. I can't be at home in my garden." Then a new empowered thought entered: "I get to have a holiday. I get to learn the healing powers of flowers. I get a break from my unhappy marriage." This thought brought relief and I saw my life in a new light.

A few days later, sitting with the cow parsnip flower, I heard, "Focus on the good. Blessings will come from this. Have faith." Reflecting on these words, I felt better. The plants were restoring me to peace each time I returned to the forest feeling distressed. I discovered a new way of thinking and felt happier. I was fast transforming and my heart filled with gratitude.

Rain came by summer's end and I returned home. However, now the smell of gasoline from a spill next door forced me to stay indoors for the next six weeks. I felt angry.

On this beautiful September morning, I felt like Job in the Bible, experiencing one severe test after another. Filled with despair, I wondered when life would feel better. I returned to the forest to visit my favorite tree, which I had named Mother Spruce.

With my back up against this giant 700-year-old Sitka spruce tree, I snuggled close to her large, protruding roots and felt wrapped in the arms of love. She listened to me and held me when I cried. She sent out a "spruce fart" (an emission of tremendous smell) to let me know I was loved. Mother Spruce is one of the most compassionate beings I have ever known.

Mother Spruce has become my dear friend, much like a pet would be a friend. Having been confined to my home, ill and isolated for many years, I sought companionship from the flowers, trees, and wildlife.

Feeling anguish, I sobbed. It brought me joy to collect flowers for my winter art projects when I created "Flower Fairies" and inspirational greeting cards, and now I couldn't. I didn't know how I would endure a long, dark winter without seeing the cheery faces of these flower friends.

After crying what felt like a thousand tears, I grew quiet! A voice in my head said,

"Focus on the good.
Blessings will come from this.
Have faith."

This same message had come to me weeks earlier from the plants, reminding me to stop feeling victimized. I had fallen back into my old pattern of "Woe is me," and they were reminding me to shift my perspective.

I reflected on those who lived in faraway cities who would never get to experience the peace, the beauty, or the magic of the rainforest. I recalled how the flowers had restored me to wholeness. Grace filled my soul.

Humbly I prayed, "God, please send me an elixir that will restore harmony to all people." The answer came, "Use the seven plants that gifted you with healing this summer." Placing a liquid extract of each plant into an amber bottle, I called it "Divine Support."

I was guided to draw a flower for each energy center in the human body, known as the chakras. Beginning with a daisy for the crown chakra, I watched with wonder as a flower angel appeared. I asked her, "Do you have a name?" I heard, "Yes, it's Celine." Tears streamed down my cheeks and awe filled me.

As the gloomy winter arrived, I would hear Angel Celine's sweet voice in the early morning. I would listen and write down what I heard. Our sweet friendship grew. Spending time with her was magical. I felt happy.

A month later, driving along an icy road, I felt scared. While singing "All is well" to calm myself, I saw a van coming straight towards me. I heard, "Rosie, go in the other lane NOW, or you're gonna die." I swerved. The van passed me on the passenger side. Shaken, I pulled off the road. "I really do have an angel who is protecting me," I thought.

My ability to feel safe and secure has grown with Celine by my side. I have grown sacred trust. Now she brings joyful people and experiences to me.

I discovered the time before sunrise is magical. One morning as I sat holding a Maui-grown protea flower, I said, "You didn't want to be thrown out, Ms. Protea. How may I serve you?" I took several slow, easy breaths and listened. I heard, "We would like you to write a book called *Think Like a Flower,* and we will dictate it to you. Would you be willing to do this?" Tears streamed down my cheeks. Sensing my doubts, the flowers continued, "We have chosen YOU because you have suffered much. When people see your fairy artwork, they will realize you are connected to us. Please do this. Pretty please."

Hearing "Pretty please," I felt a tug at my heart and replied, "Okay." I wasn't sure what I was getting into. I wondered, "If I don't do this, will I regret it?"

As I wrote each morning, a magical journey unfolded. After two weeks the flowers asked me to go to Maui to make a flower remedy called Beautiful.

"Impossible" is what I kept saying to the flowers and Celine each time they brought it up. I argued, "I haven't been on a plane in thirteen years. You know my physical limitations." The next six weeks I woke each night feeling scared. Celine would comfort me as I trembled with fear.

The stress in my marriage escalated. I heard, "You are not ready to write a book." I felt doubt. Returning to my bedroom, I'd talk to Celine. Her picture hung on my wall with the words "I am succeeding. Celine is on my side." I knew my life would get better with an angel on my side. This was a test for me to believe in me!

Each night before sleep I'd write down how I was supported by the Divine. At first, my list was short, but as I persevered, my list grew. After a month of this practice I was writing a page a night. My trust in God's beautiful plan for me increased. I was growing trust. I was going to Maui to make the remedy Beautiful, and for the first time I stood up to my husband.

With Celine's help I discovered my lost voice. I had been molested when I was five, and I didn't know how to say "Stop!" A pattern had been started in which I couldn't speak my truth to men. No matter if their actions or words hurt, I kept the peace, which hurt me.

There is a deeper learning here as well. My other attempts to leave my husband had not been successful. Now I realize that in order to start a new life, I had to reclaim my power, by speaking my truth to him.

Celine has helped me see hurting people lash out and hurt. They are acting unconsciously — speaking and acting out of pain, damage, or ignorance. I have learned compassion for my former husband and for myself. I am grateful to him for being my greatest teacher.

As a result, magic now follows me. As I take leaps of faith, Celine lends me her wings so I can soar. I landed safely on Maui. I remain in paradise because I keep asking, "God, what is your beautiful plan here?" I dwell in possibilities instead of despair. A beautiful life has unfolded for me as I focus on the good. I see each situation as an opportunity to evolve into a more loving person. Like attracts like, and as I become more loving, more love flows to me. A pansy or a daisy has just one eye; it sees with love and this is my wish.

Learning to think like a flower, I attract opportunities, much like a flower attracts bees. I have more love in my life than I could ever have imagined and have become prosperous beyond my wildest dreams.

Do you believe the Divine does things to you or for you? Do you believe the Divine loves and supports you? I invite you to pause for a moment to reflect on this.

Can you open to the possibility that the Divine does things for you? Perhaps your marriage is not easy, which is causing you to search for solutions and grow in new ways. Are you willing to see — everything is happening for your highest good?

My story illustrates that even when my life looked horrible it was indeed for my highest good and was a purification process I had to go through to bring my gifts forth. If I had not become ill, I would not have discovered the healing power of the flowers. If I had not lived in the forest, I may not have asked for an elixir to restore harmony. My journey demonstrates how much Mother Earth loves and supports you and me! She has sent us an angel named Celine.

The Divine is greater than anything I can fathom. I have grown sacred trust in the invisible world, that a beautiful plan is indeed unfolding. During these uncertain times, with help I can embrace the unknown. I can walk in faith, with help from the plants and angel Celine.

My elixir "Divine Support," opens blocked energy pathways so you can feel your connection to the Divine and hear your soul's wisdom! It's like connecting to the right radio station, so you can hear the Divine's beautiful plan for your life. The plants are offering you courage and faith to fulfill your dreams. Connecting and opening to the Divine, you receive all you require to live a happy soulful life.

Whatever your circumstances, even if you feel no hope, I invite you to reach out to Angel Celine for help. I was ill for a long time and unhappily married. Angel Celine helped me become well and free. Celine has raised me up to be more than I could have imagined.

If I can do this with Angel Celine's help, you can too! I hope you make positive changes in your life and become happier as a result.

Rosie Quigley is a soul-alchemist and truth-seeker. By following signs from the Divine, she is unraveling the mysteries of life and love. Having spent close to two decades ill and confined to her home, she learned to tap into the invisible world for strength and encouragement. The flowers revealed secrets that helped her get well. Rosie desires to nurture you so you can expand and connect to your powerful, authentic, divine self. Meet Angel Celine at www.AngelCeline.com.

Safari into the Soul

Mia Rose

THE TILES WERE COLD BUT I WAS COLDER, slumping on the floor of the shower in a small house with a sea view in Yeppoon, a coastal town at the foot of the Great Barrier Reef. Moments before, I'd washed down a few sleeping pills with a glass of Chardonnay. I was surprised at the heaviness of my limbs, though I'd been spiraling down into a black hole for a few months and by now was on intimate terms with the weight of despair.

I was tired. I was naked. I was forty years old. And if I knew anything about myself it was that I was utterly isolated and alone. Miserable as I was, it seemed that I had simply woken up one morning on a strange planet in a distant galaxy where no one was hearing me and no one could understand what I was going through.

In the years prior to my sleeping pill party, I worked hard at trying not to disappoint anyone. I was a gifted student, and being successful meant pleasing my parents, teachers, and the world at large. I was fairly young when I got married, and gave birth to three girls in rapid succession. I was a qualified teacher, but I didn't really like to teach. I was a registered psychologist, but I didn't particularly enjoy having close and intimate encounters with people all day long. I felt trapped in a career in which I excelled, but which didn't bring me much satisfaction.

I was dimly aware that my life had lost meaning; that I was out of touch with my calling. My dream was to transition from being a full-time therapist to being a full-time writer. My existence felt spiritless and dull, and I craved a different kind of life. There were mysterious places in my soul that I had never allowed myself to explore, and I wanted to know all of me – all that I was capable of.

To find clarity and discover my purpose, I knew I had to visit my roots. I planned a trip to Africa, the place of my birth. I decided to spend my time at Mantobeni, one of the Honeyguide Tented Safari Camps in the 23,000-hectare Manyeleti Game Reserve. I wasn't sure what I would find there, but I was hoping to navigate my way back to my soul, to find insight where blindness and despair had taken hold. I didn't hear life's rhythm anymore and had no idea how to move along with life's joyous dance.

I sat quietly in the plane, gazing at the peculiar abstract patterns on the endless golden-brown African plains beneath me – the winding vein of a river, clumps of trees, a few single-track roads snaking their way across the flat, featureless bush, and the weighty purple hills in the distance.

I made a simple commitment to myself to slow down to the pace of Africa; to make the shift from doing to being; to be true to myself and my surroundings; to listen to my body – eat when I was hungry and sleep when I was tired; to focus on my senses and breathe the fresh air deeply and consciously. Like any proper safari, this was to be a journey of discovery.

We descended from a crisp, blue autumn sky, and Hein, one of the friendly rangers, met us at the Hoedspruit airstrip. As soon as we turned off to Manyeleti, meaning "Place of the Stars," the quality of the dirt road rapidly deteriorated as we crashed along towards the camp. At Khoka Moya we changed vehicles and made the final trek to Mantobeni in one of the open Landrovers used for game-tracking drives.

It was April and unusually hot. When we stepped out of the vehicle we were met with a calm silence that inexplicably made me feel not only at home, but enveloped in serenity. The camp was set among tamboti trees on the banks of a riverbed. The setting sun bathed the foliage in a warm glow, with every shape and texture accentuated by the long rays.

The building was elegant in its simplicity, the palette consisting of crushed ochre, amber, and gold. Soft shadows danced against the canvas screens hanging from the roof. From the sundeck of the swimming pool, one could watch wild game like elephants visiting the nearby waterhole.

No walking alone after dark, I was told. Predators, the four-legged kind, often entered the camp at night. Hein needn't have worried – I was more than happy to be escorted by a ranger. For extra protection I was given a whistle. I was supposed to blow it loudly when I needed assistance, but not, said Hein with a twinkle in his eyes, when I merely wanted a cup of tea.

Home to me for the next few days was a tent with unrestricted views of the bush. A rustic leather couch dominated a private veranda in front of the tent. As soon as I was alone, I stumbled across a massive spider in the bathroom. I briefly wondered if this was a whistle moment, but then decided my embarrassment at being afraid of a spider was worse than my fear. I grabbed the nearest magazine, took a deep breath, and gently helped it out of the tent.

My mind needed rest even more than my body. My bed was a soft white cloud that allowed uninterrupted vision of the bush through a transparent insect screen. As soon as I succumbed to the fresh cotton sheets and down duvet, my body relaxed into sleep. I woke up at 2:00 a.m. to the rhythmic sounds of night in Africa: crickets, frogs, the muffled hoots of an owl, and occasionally a lion roaring in the distance. I happily drifted back into slumber.

It was still dark outside when African drums announced the start of the day. A sunny face appeared at the tent flap, carrying a tray with rooibos tea and a plate of biscuits. After a quick wash in the open-air shower, I pinched a few minutes to journal, but found that my mind was still and my fingers lazy, though my senses were wide awake. The trees around me were alive with the chatter of a dawn chorus of birds, the tall grass lit golden-green with the first rays of the sun. I felt completely in tune with nature.

I allowed my heart to do my thinking for a while. Who had I become? I wondered. What made me feel deeply content? What was my life purpose? I became aware of a deep desire to forge an intimate relationship with the natural world that surrounded me. Right there, that solitude, that sense of peace, was all I needed.

At about 6:00 a.m. I set out on a bush walk led by Hein and our tracker, Famuel. We walked in single file, flattening the long, wet grass with our feet and jumping over mounds of fresh elephant dung like children playing hopscotch. At Skybed Dam we stood still for a while, captivated by the sight of seven huge hippos in the water. The bull hippo focused on us, displayed his awesome jaws, snorted, and started moving in our direction. Hein and Famuel remained alert but relaxed, assuring us that the hippos were likely to stay in the water where they felt safe. By 9:00 a.m. sweat was trickling down my spine and my shirt felt too tight across my chest. It was time to head back to camp.

On every game drive a feeling of freedom and space captivated me. Everything seemed magnified and slowed down. Even when driving for hours on end, there was always the lure to see around the next bend. I kept an eye out for the grey hornbill that gave Mantobeni its name, but had to be content with taking a photo of a red-billed hornbill, a common sight around the camp.

We frequently happened upon small family parties of crested francolins crossing the road. As the Landrover approached them, they protested loudly and climbed high above the grass in a vigorous flapping flight before slowly gliding back to the ground. We viewed ground squirrels, a banded mongoose, baboons, nyala, bushbuck, waterbuck, and of course the ever-present impala.

One of my favorite moments was spotting a few giraffes, their long necks swaying gracefully as they moved around the trees. Hein stopped the vehicle and invited me to walk towards them. Behind me the sun had turned a fiery orange. I watched, entranced, until the giraffes moved out of sight.

That night as the sun sank on the horizon, the sky glowed a brilliant pink. The moon was already up. Famuel noticed a pride of lions lying low in the grass quite close to the road. He suggested that we stop a few hundred meters away in the hope that they would start moving. About ten minutes later, we returned to find seven lionesses on the road with a large, blond-maned lion following close by. We followed the pride for about an hour in the direction of the camp, then lost them as they disappeared into the bush.

I discovered that in order to get in touch with my purpose, I had to breathe deeply and slow down to the pace of the African bush. There was a natural rhythm to the sounds of nature and the silence. To hear it, I needed to get out of my head and into my senses.

It wasn't easy to stop thinking, but as long as thoughts reigned, feelings took hold and pulled me back into the past. Suddenly I found that words poured spontaneously through me and out of my fingers onto the keyboard of the little laptop that had become my constant companion. I wrote about what I loved and explored ways to offer that to the world. My musings always circled back to writing, to connection, to significance. I knew I wanted to be of service to the world.

On my last morning in the bush, I went for a long walk into the heart of the Mopane forest. I picked up one of the beautiful butterfly-shaped leaves as a reminder to let go of all the things I had been hiding and denying, the things I needed to take responsibility for, the things I needed to forgive. With honesty came release and with release came answers: who I was, what I wanted, and how I was now better equipped to move into a new season of my life.

Being in the midst of so much beauty made me want to be accountable for my own journey. I lost the need to blame others for anything that ever happened to me. I was willing to stop punishing myself and became willing to forgive. Only love flowed out from me and love was all that returned.

I breathed in the rush of the river, the feel of the wind on my face. I became aware of a center of wisdom within myself, far greater than I had ever been aware of. This was what I was born to do — experience all of life, connect with my source, grow in understanding about life and how it works, and transform all the complexity of living into the simple joy of inhaling and exhaling, one breath at a time. I truly saw how insignificant so many of the issues in my life were. All I could possibly need I had in that moment.

Boarding the plane back to Australia brought a new wave of self-declaration. I felt a reluctant gladness to re-enter my life. I was grateful for the insights that had dawned on me. I saw that changing course sometimes takes as much strength as fighting for the life you have.

True strength is to listen to the wisdom in your own heart, to hear the underlying harmony, and to write your own script.

The past few years have seen me grow more peaceful and content. My definition of *possible* has broadened remarkably, as has my ability to pursue those possibilities with calm assurance. I believe in a bright future again.

I say the words out loud: I believe – I believe. Everything seems to be built upon those two words, those fragile sounds like the snorting of wildebeest in full flight.

Yes. I believe.

Dr. Mia Rose is the founder of The Soulwoman Sanctuary and the editor-in-chief of Soulwoman eMagazine. Mia is a prize-winning author and psychologist with over twenty years of experience in helping people find their life purpose and master the spiritual practice of health, wealth, and happiness. She is a powerful voice in modern spirituality and shares her inspirational message about the beauty of love with a global audience at www.SoulwomanSanctuary.com.

The Vision of Transformation

Jeff Saxton

SOME PEOPLE SEEM TO ALWAYS KNOW what they want to be when they grow up. Not me. As a young teenager I never really had a clue what my purpose was. I was a shy, overly sensitive, aloof kid with never more than one close friend. I was horrified of groups. I tended to want to just stay invisible on the fringes when I was at school.

That's why I think it is so hilarious that I ended up doing youth work for a profession. But when you think about it, many people feel inferior and have low self-esteem, so actually my own teen experience was great preparation for my future. I eventually graduated with a degree in youth ministry and started working in a small church. During that time I became confident and grew in skills and experience. I loved the simplicity of pouring my life into the handful of students who were part of our congregation. I didn't care about being a big star on the stage in a big church. I was completely fulfilled in my small church ministry and never happier in my life.

The Big Offer

In the 1990s I got a call to interview for the position of assistant youth pastor at a very large church in the Midwest. It was considered a mega-church, with over 3,500 weekly attendees. The youth ministry had well over 600 people on their weekly attendance roster, and they had dozens and dozens of adult volunteers. There were two full-time youth pastor positions at this church; now they wanted to hire someone to be the assistant youth pastor to the new senior youth pastor.

I was torn. I had been content for a long time working at the small church, but eventually I knew I needed a change. I felt like this was an opportunity that someone as young as I would probably never come across again. But I wanted it to be the right thing for me. I accepted the position, moved everything I had, and began a whole new life.

Needless to say, working at a large church has some perks. First of all it was a blast to have big crowds. There are a number of things you can do with large crowds that don't work as well with smaller ones. Also, the high energy is contagious in a larger ministry. The other youth pastor and I were both high octane guys! We just kind of overflowed with creative juices and way too much vision for one ministry. It seemed that new ministries, outreaches, ideas, and programs were being birthed out of our youth ministry every month.

To keep these new ministries going we needed to enlist and equip as many adult volunteers as possible. So we began spending more and more time and energy equipping adult volunteers, basically multiplying our capability to serve. And it seemed like the more we equipped, the more the volunteers came out of the woodwork to help. It was all wonderful, at first. Everything grew and grew.

Maintaining The Strain

But after a few years of this non-stop pace, I started to feel the strain. To make matters worse, the other youth pastor and I were burning out and expressing that burnout to the senior pastor. He was indeed concerned, and not in any way causing or creating the weariness; in many ways it was our own fault. What I know now is that burnout in a mega-church environment is sometimes the inevitable result of growth. It is the fruit of proper planning, structure, pastoral care, and a lot of hard work by an incredible team of talented church members and volunteers.

Great growth is what everyone dreams about. But when that growth occurs, so does the stress. We eventually called our ministry "the monster." Once it grew to a certain size, it began to demand more and more of our energy, time, and resources. It was thrilling and also horribly taxing at the same time. The senior youth pastor had a family, so his burnout was all the more complicated. Since I was his assistant, he logically handed some of his work over to me. I was single at the time so I was happy to try to take on the extra work. Still, it all was coming to a head.

I was getting cranky and impatient with my volunteers. Sometimes I became upset over the slightest detail that was dropped, phone call that wasn't made, or visitor who wasn't followed up with. I was under great stress to get all of these details accomplished. Our daily planners looked like NFL playbooks with sometimes over fifty details needing to be done each day, and we both had full-time secretaries who were also working overtime to help us accomplish them.

Who Lays The Eggs?

I was meeting with my volunteers only in order to get work done by them. It was as if they were the geese laying the golden eggs, and I was taking as many eggs as I could without taking time to feed the geese that were laying them. I needed them only for what I could get out of them. After all, couldn't they see how stressed we were as youth

155

pastors? How dare they drop the ball! Some of them were putting in close to thirty hours a week for our youth ministry outside of holding down full-time jobs! Later I was told by some of them that they had considered quitting many times because of the pressure. Once the burnout was in full swing, it seemed like there was nothing I could do about it.

The only way to avoid burnout is to change. Unfortunately it took me some time to discover that the change needed was not an outward change but an inward one that comes from an internal decision to be personally transformed.

Outwardly our youth ministry was being emulated and admired by many, and we were getting invited to speak at conferences and seminars about youth ministry. But inwardly all was not well. We were only getting more and more exhausted. I was personally spending sixty-plus hours a week or more in my role. Soon I was near the breaking point. The church at large was experiencing similar strains. Many of the other staff pastors were going through considerable stress as well caused by the addition of more parishioners and their needs. In our church there was never one scandal or sin, just very tired ministers!

And then one day I was seriously too tired to go any farther. I knew I was in trouble. I was resenting my job and dreaming about getting out of it altogether. It was then that I cried out to God for help.

Divine Alignment

I went on a retreat at a hotel and spent some time praying, fasting, and thinking. The powerful thing about fasting is that it tends to remove selfishness from the equation when seeking guidance and wisdom or just trying to get your head right. Nothing came to me at first, but after a few hours I really opened up on the inside. I took a good hard look at myself and asked God to show me what He wanted to show me.

I realized that my heart had changed in the last year or two; there were misplaced priorities and secret personal ambitions driving me that were not focused on others. Some of my dreams and aspirations became more and more selfish. With success comes the temptation to think selfishly and vainly about almost everything. And when you have 3,500 people thinking you are a rock star, it can go to your head.

I decided to get right with God and what He had told me in the beginning of my calling. My life was to be one of purpose, of helping others succeed. I was supposed to be serving others rather than getting others to serve me. I decided to get back to that simple joy of just loving God and loving a few students, just like I had in my first church position.

Once again I felt renewed and refreshed by God. I felt His spirit again and I was excited to go back to ministry and do things the right way.

What Do You See?

When I returned from my retreat, I shared what was happening to me with one of my adult volunteers. At that moment another amazing revelation came to me. It was actually a vision that I saw in my mind's eye, and it was to transform everything I did from then on. I would say it was the great life-changing vision of my life. It was the clichéd "paradigm shift" kind of vision.

I am a huge football fan — always have been and probably always will be. Football has given me valuable lessons that I relate to my life. So as I was talking with one of my volunteers at the local Taco Bell, I saw a football field in my mind. As a minister, I had always *seen* myself as the player in the middle of the field with my leaders and the people in the crowd as my fans cheering me on. I looked into the eyes of one of my leaders, Dave, and saw a 180-degree shift happen before me. It was as if everything behind this guy spun around, and suddenly I was now on the sidelines and Dave was the player on the field!

I looked at him with an unexplainable empathy, and felt an emotion similar to what new fathers might feel, or what some coaches describe as a love for their players that wells up from within them. I must confess I had never felt this kind of emotion to this degree before. I do know that whatever changes Dave sensed within me, he liked my new attitude, passion, and compassion. All who were part of my volunteer team admitted that they could see that a big positive change had happened inside of me. They suddenly felt cared for and appreciated. That was because I suddenly did care for them, and appreciated them in greater ways than ever before!

I began to read book after book about equipping leaders. I read about great selfless leaders like Abraham Lincoln, Jesus, and Mother Teresa, all who seemed to understand that they came to serve others and not to be served. I read books about coaches like John Wooden, Bobby Bowden, and Tom Osborne, who found their greatest successes when at long last they put selfish ambition behind and began to truly love and care for their players.

Less Is More

This 180-degree shift was monumental for me in regard to my daily schedule. It totally recreated my work, my skill sets, my routine, and my priorities. I began to be a coach and mentor to these volunteers. I became a true equipper. I dreamed about helping people identify their greatest strengths and passions, and then sought to fit them into roles that were tailor-made for them yet also much needed in the work as a whole.

Before, I was meeting with them SO THAT the work would get done. Now I was meeting with them FOR THEM, and somehow the work still got done! As a matter of fact, the work multiplied!

Before, they were doing what they were told and following orders, but the responsibility was mainly still on my shoulders. Now I began to give them responsibility, and they naturally took care of all those details without my asking them!

The great irony is that as I began to stop working so hard, more and more was getting done! I was changing everything and was now a coach to a bunch of youth pastors. Before, I delegated details. Now I delegated authority. I have since learned that this shift in perception is a major principle in unleashing a whole new level of success in many kinds of endeavors.

And what I also found was this: Somehow I became known for attracting many of the best adult volunteers in our church. Of course it was not because of me personally, but rather it was the result of deciding to be a selfless, transformational agent in my world. The best and most talented people don't want to work in an environment in which they are not cared about, nurtured, and equipped. The best look for a selfless mentor who will allow them to be the best they can be. And they look for a leader who is not intimidated by their gifts and talent, yet rather enjoys when they receive success or acclaim.

Build Them For Success

If you want the best, you need to create an atmosphere in which the best are able to be all they can be.

I truly believe that no matter what vocation you are in, this revolutionary *paradigm* holds true. Whether you are a coach, teacher, leader, CEO, manager, boss, or even a parent, you can experience this same 180-degree shift of perception. As you focus less on your own needs and desires and more on the needs of those whom you lead, you can see similar results over time. Building leaders may take more time than some are willing to invest, but this is shortsighted. Over the long haul, those leaders that we have invested in will multiply our efforts.

I am convinced that without the simple revelation that I had become the coach rather than the player, much of what I have done would not have happened, and many would have missed out on a life-changing principle that has been passed along to others.

When I first graduated from college I thought that my life's work was always going to be centered on spending time with young people. Today I can see that God used that time in my life to also help me learn how to truly transform ordinary volunteers into great leaders.

Jeff Saxton has worked as a youth and family minister for almost two decades helping churches and adults transform young people into caring adults. He is the author of *The New Pharisee*, a screenwriter, an actor, and a film and stage director. He wrote, directed, and produced the feature film *Heart of the City,* and is a member of the Telly Awards' Silver Council. Jeff resides with his lovely wife in Minnesota. To connect with Jeff, visit his blog at www.JeffSaxton.wordpress.com.

Out of the Darkness and Then Some

Marcia Ullett, MA, LMFT, CPC

REMEMBER WHEN YOU WERE A CHILD and played ball with the other kids? I'm sure you recall that feeling of having the wind knocked out of you. What about the adult equivalent of finding yourself paralyzed on the floor wondering how you got there? It's like your soul is in jeopardy and you don't know which way to turn.

Do you ever wonder what happened to your dreams for yourself? Are you discouraged because you can't even remember what they were? All you know is that one day you woke up and felt like you couldn't go on; that something had to change... but what?

You're not alone. I know exactly how you feel. It's a staggering sensation, and it takes a bit before you can even get your bearings. Nothing seems okay and you wonder what's wrong with your life. How on earth did things get this way? If you really yearn for things to be different, hang in there.

I have been brought to my knees twice in my life. Both times weren't very pretty, but the extraordinary part about it is how gracefully my life was impacted. Without these experiences I would not be the person I am today, nor would I have the incredible life I have today — one that I try to live to the max. I had no idea that out of such pain could come so much awakening and such beauty.

Don't give up. You can find the answers if you really want to. Here's how I did it.

* * *

It was September of 1987, and I was desperately depressed, lonely, and scared to death. I was skinny and pale, jumpy and negative. I was addicted to drugs and alcohol and honestly didn't know where to turn. At the time I didn't realize what the problem was. I was full of blame and fear. I was walking around with a dark cloud guiding me. I felt like nothing in my life was working. It was even hard to get out of bed in the morning. All I knew was that I wasn't okay... not even close. I was so alone and so confused.

It had started innocently enough. During the 1970s I experimented with drugs and alcohol like everyone else. But since alcoholism runs in my family, I had a predisposition to become an alcoholic. Years later when all my friends stopped drinking, I could not. I kept thinking I could control it or cut down, but neither of these efforts worked. As my addiction progressed, my life spiraled beyond my control.

For years I had no idea that I was living by default, just trying to make up my life as I went along. Nor did I understand what living with any kind of purpose meant. I floated impulsively from page to page and chapter to chapter in my life story. I felt so desperately insecure, yet it never sunk in that it was my job to make choices regarding the course of my life and to consider each decision carefully. I needed to look at the big picture as well as all the smaller ones that made up the days, weeks, and months of my life. I simply woke up in the morning and said something like "Okay, today I want this or that." There was no framework to these moments, and I felt so out of control. I think one of the reasons I did so well in school was that I loved the structure. I felt safe in school. Otherwise the world seemed far too big and I felt far too small.

I had no touchstone – nothing to assure me that everything was going to be alright. I sought a spiritual path, hoping to emerge from the darkness that was engulfing me. I even learned to meditate with the Maharishi. But meditation couldn't lift me out of the doldrums as long as I was using alcohol and drugs. Denial is a really sneaky partner; it prevented me from seeing what was happening to me.

When my schooling was done, I began working as a therapist intern by day, but I was into drugs and alcohol by night. Every morning I would step into the world, into the light, and it was so frightening for me that I had to run back into the darkness of getting high. I was living a double life, and I was having trouble keeping track of it and myself.

It was at this time that the Universe presented me with the idea of sobriety. My first client in my internship was a recovering alcoholic who was very proud of his ten years of sobriety and couldn't wait to tell me all about it. He had come to me for relationship issues; he had no idea how much his presence in my office helped me. I saw the light in his eyes and knew I needed that if I were to live. Before I knew it, I met a group of people who had been through much of what I had. These people knew the pain and terror of addiction and had learned to live sober lives. They saved my life and, over time, taught me to love and accept myself.

Gradually I began to see everything through different eyes, grateful for every moment of my new life. I had to learn to surrender to many new ideas because nothing I had known was working for me. The more I accepted life as it was rather than fighting to get my way, the more my heart began to warm up and breathe new life into my soul. I learned to be responsible and accountable for my life. My recovery was slow but consistent. Most important of all was my emerging belief in a God of my understanding – a faith that literally rocked my world and grew with every passing day.

* * *

It was February of 2002, and I had settled into a nice life working in a treatment center for adolescents and their families and in my own small private practice. I was going to meetings to support my sobriety and spending time helping other alcoholics as well as time with family and friends. The clients in my private practice were getting better, wanting more. More? More what? We worked on emotional issues, often from their past, that impacted them in their daily lives. They felt hopeful and wanted to go forward, yet they wanted more than that. I wasn't sure what that meant. I felt unprepared to help them and started to feel confused about my own purpose.

That was when I found the lump. *It couldn't be,* I thought. But that little voice inside of me said, *It is.* Sure enough – breast cancer. Of course I panicked. I sat on my living room floor for hours and imagined all the worst scenarios. My body had turned on me. I felt so betrayed. I had been eating right and exercising regularly for fifteen years by now, and to what avail? I felt hot and dizzy, as though I would burst into flames. Again my life suddenly felt like I was at the mercy of forces I didn't understand. I felt like my feminine soul was under attack. I actually began to shake uncontrollably as I sat there until long after it got dark outside. I was so scared and angry. I thought about drinking. Cancer certainly seemed like the perfect excuse. Maybe I could drink... at least it would allow me to forget for a while.

I drifted off into space when suddenly the doors of my pity party slammed shut and I saw my life instead. I pictured my family and friends, the love I had in my life, and my progress over all those years. Did I really want to throw all that away... because I was scared? I had certainly been scared before. I had tools for dealing with that. I had a Higher Power on whom I had come to depend. Exhausted, I began to meditate. After a while I got up and started to reach out for support. Not only did I want to stay sober, but I was going to have to find a way to embrace survival once again — this time at a whole new level. I began to meditate regularly, and I prayed for the willingness to do this new recovery with all my strength.

I realized then that willingness is the key to moving forward in any way. If you're faced with a challenge that threatens to flatten you, pray for the willingness to do whatever you're called to do. And once you feel it, it will be clear to you what you need to do, and both your eyes and your heart will be opened, making it possible to take action. It has been said that once you make a decision about something, the Universe opens its arms and begins to send help. That's exactly what happened to me. Not that it was easy, but it was possible. I could now sense a way to move through this difficult and painful time.

The treatment for cancer was rugged and took about three months. I continued to work, but the rest of my life slowed down so that I could rest. Resting led to some realizations. My view of the world was changing again. I was becoming more accepting of things in general. After all, I couldn't control cancer; I couldn't control fear. And guess what? I can't control life either. But I can manage it to some degree if I am willing to surrender to the truth. And the truth was becoming abundantly clear. I was cooperating with the solution for my life just as so many women before me had done and would do after me. I was a woman among women and simply needed to do what was in front of me.

Had you asked me fifteen years earlier if I considered my life to be precious to me, I would have laughed. All I really wanted then was for it to be livable, and to be shown how to crawl out of the darkness. Yet there I was, all those years later, willing to do *anything* to keep what I had been given.

I'm sure that you've heard and read many stories about people whose lives changed as a result of some crisis that could have killed them. I guess that was what was happening to me. I could see how precious life is while at the same time how fragile. It needed to be cherished each day, every minute.

Once treatment was over and I was strong again, I took a long look at my life. I remembered that my clients had been asking for more from me now that their issues were being handled. I had to find out what they meant. I hired a life coach to help me, and soon realized that some of his tools would be useful – tools that help you find new goals in life, such as beginning with your values and envisioning the next chapter of your life. These tools helped me find new meaning. I felt an urgency to move forward in my life, and I had a tremendous amount of renewed energy.

I entered a postgraduate program for executive coaches. I learned many new concepts, but the one that stood out for me was *purpose*. I had never really thought much about living purposefully, and I began to imagine where that might lead. What would it be like to have a higher purpose that burned within me? Would it broaden and deepen my life? My work? Maybe that was what my clients were asking of me. I began to study purpose.

What purpose began to mean to me is a whole new way of looking at the path in front of me. Purpose gives new meaning to everything I do. It motivates me, helps me put a meaningful frame around my life, and fills me with hope. It allows me to be really me – to be true to myself in ways that are important to me. Having a purpose helps me get deep into myself and live my life based on my most important values.

I began to wonder whether it is necessary to have a crisis in order to move in this direction. Does everyone have to walk through fire in order to find this kind of meaning, or was that just my path? Perhaps deep meaning can come out of finding your purpose whether or not a life crisis has occurred.

My clients began to do the work of living with purpose – envisioning their lives going forward. I realized that I was living my purpose – teaching others how to discover their purpose, writing about it, and teaching it to therapists, coaches, and counselors so that they can use it with their clients.

During most of my life I did not know how to find my purpose, nor did I even think about such things. Having a purpose that burns within me allows me to stretch beyond my fears. I feel really passionate about my life now. Most days I'm excited to get up and follow this passion. I think sometimes about how much fear I have experienced in my life and how getting through it has empowered me.

Today I have been sober for twenty-five years and free from cancer for ten years. I feel healthy and strong. Looking back I realize that being willing to get through the hottest fire is necessary because life on the other side is like experiencing a cool breeze wash over me. It has filled me with new hope. Everything I have been through has led me, like a funnel, to finding my sense of purpose and meaning for my life. What I've received is this amazing life I get to lead. I feel deeply committed to helping others live by their values and find their purpose so they can experience their most amazing lives.

Marcia Ullett, MA, LMFT, CPC is a licensed psychotherapist and certified professional coach. While her professional experience has impacted thousands of lives, Marcia's own *life* experience is a living, breathing example of how to move out of the darkness and into a life filled with purpose, light, and gratitude. Her book *Your Best Life Yet* is set for release in 2013. Please visit www.MarciaUllett.com to get her free report, "Having It All: The Fine Art of Balancing Your Life."

It's Not About You

Neale Donald Walsch

I'VE LEARNED THAT MY WORK IN THE WORLD is not about me at any level; it's about the message that was offered to me to send to the world. My story, in brief, is really quite simple.

I had reached the lowest point of my life, where nothing was working. My relationship with my significant other had fallen apart, my livelihood had utterly and completely disappeared, my health was rapidly going downhill, and then, to make matters worse, I had an automobile accident in which I broke my neck.

I realized at that juncture that I did not want to live my life anymore in the way I had been living it. I knew that something important had to change. I just didn't know what it was, specifically, nor did I know how to do it, and I became more and more frustrated as my life went further and further downhill.

After I had my accident, I wound up living on the streets because I ran out of government social benefits. I dropped through the safety net that our society puts up for people who are in trouble. And, finally, I wound up with no money at all, thinking, "Well, this is just a temporary setback. This will just be for a week or two — a couple of months at best — and I'll get myself back on my feet." But I never got to that place in that period of time. It took me a year to get myself back together. And that year that I spent on the street was one of the most extraordinary and important periods of my life.

The *most* extraordinary event of my life, however, occurred *after* I got *off* the streets. I finally found a part-time job. Part of the problem was that I couldn't work at a normal job because I had a broken neck. I was walking around with a Philadelphia collar, a therapeutic device, and no one would hire me because they saw that I was obviously having severe health problems and they did not want any insurance claims filed by me once I started working with their company. All they could see was a person who was broken and was unable to do much heavy lifting or hard work. I could push a pencil, but that was about it, and there weren't any pencil pushing jobs available at that time. So I was largely just unemployable.

Then I finally got a little part-time weekend job at a local radio station as an on-air personality, and I thought, "Well, okay. Fair enough. I'm now off and running back into the world of work." Sure enough, that part-time job turned into a full-time job at the radio station about four months later, and I thought, "Okay. Life is going to work out."

That's when I really hit the skids, psychologically speaking, because after getting back into the swing of things I was confronted with the utter emptiness of my life. There I was again, working full-time, in some cases ten, twelve, and even fourteen hours a day, coming home exhausted. I was just making enough money to pay my bills and keep a roof over my head while putting some food in the table, but not much else. And I thought to myself, "Wait a minute. Is this really all there is? Is it just about day-to-day, week-to-week, month-to-month survival? Is that all there is to life? And the one with the most toys in the end wins?" Because if that's all there was, then I didn't want to play anymore. If life had no greater meaning than that and no greater purpose, no greater goal or objective, I just don't want to do this anymore.

I was fifty years old and had been on this planet a half century and I couldn't find any larger reason or purpose for existing. That's when I woke up one morning at 4:15 upset with life, with God, with my whole situation, looking forward to another twenty years or more of pointless activity. And so I called out to God, "What does it take to make life work?" There I was, sitting on the couch in my living room, feeling very frustrated and at odds with the world.

Just before I fell asleep on the sofa I heard a voice. I could swear that it was right in the room with me, as it was a physical sound, a physical voice, asking me if I was ready to really hear the answers to my questions. And I awoke hearing that voice, absolutely certain there was someone in the room with me. Of course, there wasn't, at least not physically.

I looked around and the voice continued, "Would you like answers to these questions?" And I thought, "Yeah, if you've got them." At first, I thought I was just talking to myself, the way we all do once in a while. Then I came to understand very quickly that I was connecting with a much higher source, because my whole physical being was filled with radiance. I hate to be sound hackneyed and so trite, but it did feel that way. I was filled with radiance, warmth, life, and light, such as to make me almost weep at the feeling of it. Tears of joy and relief streamed down my face all the while as I was sitting on my sofa at that early hour of the morning.

So I began to write my questions out. "What does it take to make life work? What's the point of all this? Somebody give me the rules. I promise I'll play. Just give me the doggone rule book! And... don't *change the rules halfway through the game.*"

Then I received all of the information that can now be found in my books. Tons and tons and tons of questions were answered. Questions I never even thought to ask were already answered.

I wound up with many, many yellow legal pads of "dictation" at the end of this period of my life. It was my habit to jot down notes, grocery lists, those sorts of things, on yellow legal pads, so I happened to have two or three lying around the house. Those three legal pads got filled up very quickly. A couple of days later I ran to the office supply store and purchased more. Before I knew it, I had fifteen or twenty of them filled with these kinds of dialogues that were now taking place on a daily basis.

I was told that these writings would one day become a book. I thought to myself, "Of course! Yes! I can see myself now, sending these pages off to a publisher telling them that God is talking to me." But, in fact, that's just what I did. I thought, "Well, you know what? This will be interesting. It will be kind of like proof this really happened to me."

I realized, of course, that publishers get 1,500+ unsolicited manuscripts a month from everyone in the world wanting to write the next great book, and they hardly open them, much less read and evaluate them, unless they come from an agent or from someone they trust. I knew my chances were slim to none. But I sent it off anyway.

Well, I was right, it seemed at first. My book of dictation notes was rejected by the four of the five publishers that I sent it to. And even the fifth publisher, the one that actually finally put it out, didn't accept it until my second sending. Their response went, "Thank you for your submission. Unfortunately, your book does not fit our titles list. We wish you well with your endeavor."

But I sent it back to that fifth publisher because I was angry. I said, "Look, you guys. You didn't even read the book. I know that because if you had read it, you could not say it did not fit your titles list, *because all you publish are metaphysical books.*"

Then I did a very daring thing. I did not send a letter with my second sending of the manuscript. All I did was tear off a page of my yellow legal pad and I scribbled on a note: "Read any ten pages!" And, you know what? The publisher took me up on the dare. Good old Bob Friedman, who has since become a good friend, picked up the book and read ten pages at random. He told me later that he immediately reached for the phone and called me.

He said, "Listen, we want to publish this book," and I was both delighted and shocked. And he did publish it. They put it on the fast track and it was published twelve to fourteen weeks after that. Three months later it landed on the *New York Times* Bestseller List, where it remained for two and a half years. That book was *Conversations With God: An Uncommon Dialogue (Book 1)*.

That's when I realized that I had something here and that when God makes promises, She doesn't kid around. She means exactly what she says.

Since that time I've continued with the process. I allowed myself to be inspired, to continue that writing and dialogue for eight more books, and for a number of follow-up texts expanding on those concepts. This allowed me to explain them more fully, as I understand them, and to share them even more deeply than I could in a simple dialogue. And that's what the twenty-seven books have produced. And I continue to write, with my latest books, *The Only Thing That Matters* published in the fall of 2012, and *What God Said*, published in autumn, 2013.

I've since realized that grace was at work in my life, that something was afoot, something much higher than I, individually and personally, could ever possibly put into place. And I realized that because the book remained on the *New York Times* list for two-and-a-half years. Ultimately, the *Conversations With God* books have reached fifteen million people in thirty-seven languages. I don't want to appear as if I'm bragging or boasting by noticing that. I'm simply indicating that's what happens when the energy is moving with a project and nothing can stop it from happening, including you.

I think that one cannot try to write a bestseller – nor can one, for that matter, try to save the planet or try to change the world. When a person fearlessly, fully, and completely enters into an expression of one's Self, of whom and what one imagines one's Self to be, then life becomes a process of expressing Oneself at the highest and grandest level that one can possibly imagine. We don't do it for the reasons of changing the world, writing a bestseller, becoming successful, or being a so-called transformational author. It's all very lovely to speak in those terms, but that isn't the ultimate purpose of it. The ultimate purpose is self-realization and self-expression, and experiencing and expressing our true identity as an aspect of the Divine. From that point, all the rest emerges automatically without an effort. Personally, I don't know how to sit down and write a bestseller, much less seven of them.

When the writing is done with none of those exterior goals in mind, then whatever happens will happen – and it will all be perfectly okay with you. Doing anything – practicing law, becoming a plumber, cleaning the floor, washing the dishes – when the "doingness" is merely an expression of the "beingness" that one has chosen to love, and when one allows that "beingness" to flow through one's self as an expression of the highest and grandest notion of who they are... *that's* the highest calling. When that's the reason one is writing, then, of course, the writing informs and serves to co-create the next expression of what one seeks to know one's Self as.

So if I seek to know myself as love, clarity, wisdom, understanding, patience, compassion, and all the other aspects of divinity that I hold dear, that I value – if that's the reason that I'm picking up the pen or putting my fingers on the keyboard, and it's not to finish the book by Thursday or somehow make a point in this particular chapter, but rather that I am writing in a flow of consciousness – then the consciousness creates the writing and then the writing creates the consciousness. This process is circular; one thing creates another, and it has no particular aim or goal except for the circular expression of "beingness" itself.

When I came to understand the reaction that people were having around the world to *Conversations with God*, one of my biggest challenges was writing the second book, as you can imagine. Because the first book was really just a free flowing-of-consciousness dialogue that I was having with God. That free flow of conscious writing continued even after what became book one was signed to be published, but then God had told me there would be three books. So I kept writing, but it was a constant process of getting myself out of the way.

If I had one piece of advice for those who want to become a transformational author, it would be to get yourself out of the way. Get out of your own personal hopes, dreams, visions, ideas, income, expectations – everything, and know that the book is not about you and somehow solving your problems, elevating your lifestyle, or whatever you imagine the book is going to do for you. If you don't or can't do that, it's going to be difficult to write it in a way that captures the human heart and expresses the mysteries of the human soul. On the other hand, if you can manage to remove yourself from the process and keep the flow moving through you from the ultimate source of wisdom in the Universe that I happen to call God, your writing will stand a much better chance of being noticed.

It took me nearly three years to complete the third book in the *Conversations With God* series. After three books in five years, I finally almost collapsed with the exertion of it. I just let go of all my expectations, including those I didn't know were there — those hidden ones under the table, the subconscious expectations.

I just said, "Okay. I'll just give all the money back. I'll just write them a check and give all the money back. I don't want to hear about the money, I don't want to hear about the fame. I don't want to hear about the so-called literary glory. I don't want to hear about the bestseller list or being on *Good Morning America* or Jay Leno. I don't want to hear about any of that. I just want to find the purity again. Help me find the purity again."

Once your path in this world has been made known to you in some way, and your being is expressing that purely in the world as you move into your role, you'll become a humanitarian — a leader if you will. Leadership is an extraordinary experience. I have been called a so-called "spiritual leader"— or one of the "leaders of the New Thought Movement." I'm not sure that's an accurate description, but I've been called that by a number of people, in the media, press, television, and so forth. So I've had to look closely at, "What is leadership?"

If you intend to be a transformational author or leader of any sort, you'll need to confront that question as well, because your work in the world may put you in what others call a place of leadership, whether you intended to be there or not. If you think that you can write a transformational book and not be thrust into a place of leadership, think again. So you need to be aware of what true leadership is, and I want to share this with you:

A leader is not one who says, "Follow me." A true leader is one who says, "I'll go first." You are going to have to demonstrate the courage, conviction, and the commitment to go first. And to go first in what? To go first in two things. First, questioning the prior assumption that you and others around you have had about everything: about money, love, God, sex, spirituality, health, everything. All the prior assumptions by which humanity lives will need to be questioned. And second, to go first in asking the great questions: "What if what I thought was so, is not so? What if I could create in my reality a different experience and a different expression of what is? What if I imagine that the whole world, every person on the planet, not just my spouse, my children, my grandchildren, my friends and neighbors, and others around me like my colleagues and associates, but every human being was watching me and using me as the model of how life could best be lived and how humanity could best be expressed? In what way, if at all, would my own behaviors change tomorrow?"

That's a huge question. The opportunity and the invitation is not to be knocked over by it, but just to live into it. If you do, your life will change overnight.

Neale Donald Walsch has written twenty-seven books on spirituality and its practical application in everyday life, the latest of which is *What God Said* (Penguin Putnam, 2013). Taken together, books in the series have been translated into thirty-seven languages, and seven of those books have reached the *New York Times* Bestseller List. Neale is also the creator of several worldwide outreach projects: The CwG Foundation, CwG for Parents, Humanity's Team, the Changing Change Network, The Global Conversation, and CWG Connect, all accessible through the internet gateway site www.CWGPortal.com, and all dedicated to helping the world move from violence to peace, from confusion to clarity, and from anger to love. Neale lives with his wife, the American poet Em Claire, in Ashland, Oregon, USA.

Become a Contributing Author
in the Next Wave of

Pebbles in the Pond:
Transforming the World One Person at a Time

If you want to share your story in the next "Wave" in this series, and believe in the powerful impact one voice (*your story*) can have on truly making a difference, I want to hear from you!

Ask any one of the authors in this book and they'll tell you that it's been a life-changing experience to be a contributing author to *Pebbles in the Pond*. Beyond the accomplishment of getting published alongside some of today's most successful authors, you'll become part of a powerful mastermind "family," or as we've come to call it – a MasterHeart.

You'll make valuable connections and life-long friendships with like-minded authors. And you'll receive eight months of guidance and coaching to help you write your chapter and get started as a Transformational Author.

You'll also work with a professional editor to polish your chapter (so don't fret if you feel your writing isn't "perfect" – nobody's is). You'll receive an additional six months of coaching in my award-winning

Get Your Book Done® program to write your *own* book, plus free attendance at the famous Transformational Author Retreat (a three-day retreat with your fellow contributors). Of course, you'll also receive your own copies of the next *Pebbles in the Pond* book – the one you will be in!

If you're interested in applying to be a contributor in the next "Wave," please email Info@ChristineKloser.com right away to get more details.

I hope to have the opportunity to work with you and see your story in our next book!

Many blessings,

Christine Kloser

Spiritual Guide ~ Award-Winning Author
Transformational Book Coach
President, Transformation Books

Connect With Christine Kloser

Website
www.ChristineKloser.com
www.PebblesInThePondBook.com

FREE Transformational Author Training
If you want help writing your *own* book, visit:
www.TransformationalAuthor.com or
www.GetYourBookDone.com

Social Media
www.Facebook.com/christinekloserfanpage
www.Facebook.com/transformationalauthors
www.twitter.com/christinekloser

Mail
Christine Kloser Companies LLC
211 Pauline Drive #513
York, PA 17402

Phone
(800) 930-3713

Email
Info@ChristineKloser.com

About Christine Kloser

Christine Kloser is a Spiritual Guide, Award-Winning Author, and Transformational Book Coach whose spot-on guidance transforms the lives of visionary entrepreneurs and authors around the world. Her passion is fueled by her own transformation in December of 2010 when, after much success as an entrepreneur, she found herself curled up in a ball on the floor sobbing because she had lost it all. When she let go of the last shred of stability and security in her life, she discovered her truth and the blessings began to flow.

From that place, she fearlessly (and faithfully) went on to create the most abundant, impactful, and joyous success of her life in a matter of a few short months as a pioneering leader of the Transformational Author movement. Christine knows how to flip the switch from "broke" to "blessed" and shares her wisdom through her books, award-winning email newsletter, speaking, coaching programs, and services.

She's been featured in the *Los Angeles Times, Entrepreneur Magazine, Atlanta Constitution-Journal, Leadership Excellence, FOX News, Forbes.com, Huffington Post,* and *Entrepreneur.com*, and is a regular columnist for the award-winning *PUBLISHED* Magazine. Her books and publications have received numerous awards including the *Nautilus Book Silver Award, Pinnacle Book Award, National Best Books Award*, and *Apex Award for Publication Excellence.*

After living in Los Angeles, California, for fourteen years, Christine now resides in York, Pennsylvania, with her husband, David, and daughter, Janet, where they enjoy a much slower-paced and relaxed lifestyle.

Learn more about Christine at *www.ChristineKloser.com.*